Swift Development for the Apple Watch

Jon Manning and Paris Buttfield-Addison

Beijing · Boston · Farnham · Sebastopol · Tokyo

Swift Development for the Apple Watch

by Jon Manning and Paris Buttfield-Addison

Printed in the United States of America.

Published by O'Reilly Media, Inc., 1005 Gravenstein Highway North, Sebastopol, CA 95472.

O'Reilly books may be purchased for educational, business, or sales promotional use. Online editions are also available for most titles (*http://safaribooksonline.com*). For more information, contact our corporate/institutional sales department: 800-998-9938 or *corporate@oreilly.com*.

Editor: Brian MacDonald	**Indexer:** Elisa Jepson
Acquisitions Editor: Rachel Roumeliotis	**Interior Designer:** David Futato
Production Editor: Nicole Shelby	**Cover Designer:** Randy Comer
Copyeditor: Molly Ives Brower	**Illustrator:** Rebecca Demarest
Proofreader: Jasmine Kwityn	

June 2016:   First Edition

Revision History for the First Edition
2016-05-25:   First Release

See *http://oreilly.com/catalog/errata.csp?isbn=9781491925201* for release details.

978-1-491-92520-1

[LSI]

Table of Contents

Preface

Apple has given developers a lot of toys to play with, and a lot of new things to learn over the past few years: iPhone, iPad, Swift, and now the Apple Watch. We've been using Swift to build OS X and iOS apps for nearly a year (and enjoying every moment of it), but now we can also use it to build apps for a tiny wrist-mounted computer—the kind of science-fiction gadget that we used to dream about as kids is now reality! We can't wait to see the apps people create for the Apple Watch.

This book introduces the basic components available to developers who want to build apps for the Apple Watch. If you're already familiar with Swift, this book has all the basics you need to get familiar with the fundamentals of Apple Watch development. If you're in the middle of learning Swift from another book or video series, this book provides an excellent resource to move to once you're familiar with Swift and ready to tackle the Apple Watch.

We hope you enjoy learning the basics of Apple Watch development with this book!

Audience

This book assumes that you already know how to use Swift. If you've worked through any other Swift-based book available from O'Reilly, like *Learning Swift*, you should be good to go with this book.

We assume that you're a relatively capable programmer who is happy and confident navigating around OS X, Xcode, and iOS, but we don't assume you know how to program for the Apple Watch (that's what this book is for!)

Organization of This Book

In this book, we'll be discussing the basics of using Apple's WatchKit framework to build watchOS apps. We'll be coding in Swift, Apple's newest programming language.

Here is a concise breakdown of the material each chapter covers:

Chapter 1 reviews what the Apple Watch is—and what it isn't. We discuss how and why people might interact with your Apple Watch app, the life cycle of an app, and how it interacts with the user's iPhone. We also briefly touch on design contraints and UI controls available for use in your Apple Watch apps.

Chapter 2 teaches you how to build an Apple Watch app and its iOS counterpart. We talk about adding controls, working with multiple screens in your app, and sharing data with iOS apps.

Chapter 3 discusses *glances*, the non-interactive component of Apple Watch apps that provides *glanceable* information to users. We will also demonstrate how to build a simple glance.

Chapter 4 covers *notifications* and the Apple Watch. We discuss creating, presenting, and customizing notifications, as well as how to test notifications and connect them to your interface controller(s).

Chapter 5 discusses *complications*, which let you embed small information displays directly into the watch face to provide timely information to the user.

Conventions Used in This Book

The following typographical conventions are used in this book:

Italic
> Indicates new terms, URLs, email addresses, filenames, and file extensions.

`Constant width`
> Used for program listings, as well as within paragraphs to refer to program elements such as variable or function names, databases, data types, environment variables, statements, and keywords.

`Constant width bold`
> Shows commands or other text that should be typed literally by the user.

`Constant width italic`
> Shows text that should be replaced with user-supplied values or by values determined by context.

 This element signifies a tip or suggestion.

This element signifies a general note.

This element indicates a warning or caution.

Using Code Examples

Supplemental material (code examples, exercises, errata, etc.) is available for download at our site (*http://www.secretlab.com.au/books/swift-development-for-apple-watch*).

This book is here to help you get your job done. In general, if example code is offered with this book, you may use it in your programs and documentation. You do not need to contact us for permission unless you're reproducing a significant portion of the code. For example, writing a program that uses several chunks of code from this book does not require permission. Selling or distributing a CD-ROM of examples from O'Reilly books does require permission. Answering a question by citing this book and quoting example code does not require permission. Incorporating a significant amount of example code from this book into your product's documentation does require permission.

We appreciate, but do not require, attribution. An attribution usually includes the title, author, publisher, and ISBN. For example: "*Swift Development for the Apple Watch* by Jon Manning and Paris Buttfield-Addison (O'Reilly). Copyright 2016 Secret Lab, 978-1-491-92520-1."

If you feel your use of code examples falls outside fair use or the permission given above, feel free to contact us at *permissions@oreilly.com*.

Finally, we'd be remiss if we didn't link to our own blog (*http://secretlab.com.au/blog*).

Safari® Books Online

 *Safari Books Online* is an on-demand digital library that delivers expert content in both book and video form from the world's leading authors in technology and business.

Technology professionals, software developers, web designers, and business and creative professionals use Safari Books Online as their primary resource for research, problem solving, learning, and certification training.

Safari Books Online offers a range of plans and pricing for enterprise, government, education, and individuals.

Members have access to thousands of books, training videos, and prepublication manuscripts in one fully searchable database from publishers like O'Reilly Media, Prentice Hall Professional, Addison-Wesley Professional, Microsoft Press, Sams, Que, Peachpit Press, Focal Press, Cisco Press, John Wiley & Sons, Syngress, Morgan Kaufmann, IBM Redbooks, Packt, Adobe Press, FT Press, Apress, Manning, New Riders, McGraw-Hill, Jones & Bartlett, Course Technology, and hundreds more. For more information about Safari Books Online, please visit us online.

How to Contact Us

Please address comments and questions concerning this book to the publisher:

O'Reilly Media, Inc.
1005 Gravenstein Highway North
Sebastopol, CA 95472
800-998-9938 (in the United States or Canada)
707-829-0515 (international or local)
707-829-0104 (fax)

We have a web page for this book, where we list errata, examples, and any additional information. You can access this page at *http://bit.ly/swift-dev-apple-watch*.

To comment or ask technical questions about this book, send email to *bookquestions@oreilly.com*.

For more information about our books, courses, conferences, and news, see our website at *http://www.oreilly.com*.

Find us on Facebook: *http://facebook.com/oreilly*

Follow us on Twitter: *http://twitter.com/oreillymedia*

Watch us on YouTube: *http://www.youtube.com/oreillymedia*

Acknowledgments

Jon thanks his mother, father, and the rest of his weirdly extended family for their tremendous support.

Paris thanks his mother, whose credit card bankrolled literally hundreds of mobile devices throughout his childhood—an addiction that, in all likelihood, created the gadget-obsessed monster he is today. He can't wait to read her upcoming novel.

Thank you to our editor, Rachel Roumeliotis, who kept the book under control and provided a ton of useful advice on content (we know it was a ton because we measured it). Likewise, all the O'Reilly Media staff and contractors we've worked with over the course of writing the book have been absolutely fantastic, and their collective efforts have made this book better. Thank you also to Brian Jepson, our first editor at O'Reilly.

A huge thank you to Tony Gray and the Apple University Consortium (AUC) for the monumental boost they gave us and many others listed on this page. We wouldn't be working in this industry, let alone writing books, if it wasn't for Tony and the AUC community.

Thanks also to Neal Goldstein, who richly deserves all of the credit and/or blame for getting both of us into the whole book-writing racket.

We'd like to thank the support of the goons at MacLab, who know who they are and continue to stand watch for Admiral Dolphin's inevitable apotheosis, as well as Professor Christopher Lueg, Dr Leonie Ellis, and the rest of the staff at the University of Tasmania for putting up with us.

Additional thanks to Tim N., Nic W., Andrew B., Jess L., and Rex S. for a wide variety of reasons. Thanks also to Ash Johnson, for general support.

Finally, very special thanks to Steve Jobs, without whom this book (and many others like it) would not have reason to exist.

CHAPTER 1

Understanding the Apple Watch

Apple describes the Apple Watch as "a new chapter in the relationship people have with technology." While it remains to be seen whether this is quite the case, the Apple Watch, as it exists right now, is a tiny programmable computer that sits on your wrist. It's even smaller than Apple's other recent tiny programmable computers.

watchOS apps are written using a framework called *WatchKit*. The code runs on the watch, but because the Apple Watch is tightly linked to the iPhone, writing apps for the Apple Watch also means writing an iOS app.

How Users Interact with Apple Watch

watchOS apps can provide four different components for the user: full apps, glances, notifications, and complications. You must always create a full Apple Watch app, which can be opened from the home screen of the Apple Watch.

- Full apps behave in a similar way to iPhone apps, and can have multiple screens and a range of possible interactions.

- Glances are single screens of content that can be accessed by swiping up from the watch face. They don't have any interactive elements—they're only for displaying information. If the user taps on the screen, the full app is launched.

- Notifications appear when the watchOS app's counterpart iOS app receives a notification. Notifications usually come from the Apple Push Notification service, but they can also be "local" notifications, which the iOS app schedules for later delivery.

- Complications are small elements that are embedded into certain watch faces. They're not interactive, but they let apps add a little more information to the most quickly accessible part of the phone's interface. Additionally, they can also participate in Time Travel, in which the user rotates the Digital Crown to view the watch face as it appeared in the past, or will appear in the future.

 The word "complication" comes from the fact that these elements on the watch face, when they were part of physical, clockwork-driven watches, were *complications* in the clockwork assembly.

How the Apple Watch Works with iPhone

watchOS apps are embedded inside iOS apps. When you download and install an iOS app that contains a watchOS app inside it, that app is automatically transferred over the Bluetooth link to the watch. If the watch isn't in Bluetooth range of the iPhone at the time, it's installed later.

watchOS apps are independent applications that run entirely on the watch: they do their own processing, manage their own memory, and can store files on the watch. However, watchOS apps rely on the parent iPhone for access to any of the user's data that's stored on the device.

 Apple Watches require the presence of a parent iPhone. They don't work without one; additionally, they specifically require an iPhone, not an iPod touch or an iPad.

App Life Cycle

Apps for the Apple Watch have a unique life cycle when compared to iOS or OS X applications. Your app can be launched in a variety of circumstances:

- When the user explicitly launches your app from the watch home screen
- When the user interacts with notifications from your app on the watch
- When the user interacts with a glance provided by your app
- When the watch face needs to update a complication on the watch face provided by your app

 The battery on the watch is significantly smaller than the one built into the phone, which means that it pays to be very careful about the work that you do on the device.

A watchOS App's Architecture

A watchOS app is very similar to an iOS app: it's a bundle of resources and code. The resources include the files that define the UI, any images and media needed by the app, and the compiled binary containing all of the app's code.

The watchOS app is exposed to the user as an icon on the Apple Watch's home screen, which is the grid of icons that you see when you press the Digital Crown from the watch face. In addition to the main app itself, a watchOS app can also include the following:

- A single *glance* interface, which allows the app to display a quick, single-page summary of the most important information. For example, when you swipe up from the bottom of the screen, you can access a quick summary of the current weather; this is a glance interface provided by the Weather app.
- Customized interfaces for each of the different types of notifications the user might receive. The Uber app customizes the presentations of notifications that alert the user when the car he has requested is arriving, to show the license plate number of the car to look for.
- A number of *complications*: small user-interface elements that are shown as part of the watch face. The Weather app also provides a small summary of the current weather, embedded directly into the watch face.

To communicate with the parent iPhone, you use the `WatchConnectivity` framework to send and receive files, or small chunks of information. `WatchConnectivity` is the only way to access information that's kept inside the iOS app—because the Apple Watch and the iPhone are separate devices, there's no shared file storage between them.

Designing for the Apple Watch

The Apple Watch requires you to think about the constraints of the device you're designing for with even more pedantry and attention to detail than is required for the iPhone and iPad. You need to keep the following in mind when designing Apple Watch apps:

- The Apple Watch has an absolutely, ridiculously minuscule screen—it's tiny!
- The screen is not visible most of the time
- Nobody wants to spend any more than five seconds, if that, looking at it
- The watch is a separate computer (more on this later)
- It has no keyboard, so the only text input available is via voice dictation

- It has a very, very small storage capacity—less than 8 GB, and only a tiny fraction of that is available for you to use

In general, as long as you're careful—and pay attention to the design constraints of the watch—you'll probably be fine if you follow the same general approach that is taken for iOS development. That said, it's easy to forget that every single thing that your Apple Watch app does relies on an often unreliable Bluetooth connection to an iPhone. It's especially easy to forget this when you're using the simulator to test things, because the Watch simulator doesn't have to deal with talking over the radio to its simulated counterpart iPhone. This means that the simulator will be significantly faster than a real Apple Watch will be.

Dealing with the Device and Simulator

There are two ways to run an Apple Watch app: running it on a real device, and running it in the simulator.

Just as with building apps for iPhone and iPad, it's always better to run your code on a real device, for a bunch of reasons: the simulator is faster than the real watch, and responds to user input much more quickly; the simulator is a lot easier to read than the real watch; and apps running on the simulator don't have to compete for attention with other apps. Additionally, when you're running code on the simulator, you're not wearing the app on your wrist, and you're not interacting with it in the same way.

At the same time, though, building and testing your app on the simulator is considerably easier than using a real device—you don't need to worry about pairing, or waiting for the install to complete. You also don't have to own a real device. (Again, though, if you're making apps, you really should own a watch. Given the cost of buying additional hardware, though, it's understandable to want to start building apps on the simulator before getting a device.)

Diving In

Let's dive into creating an app for the Apple Watch. Because we're starting from scratch, the iOS app that runs on the phone will be mostly empty, and we'll focus our attention on the watchOS app.

To get started, you'll need a copy of Xcode 7.2 or later installed.

When shipping a real app, your iOS app needs to be fully functional. Focus on getting that product complete *as well as* your Apple Watch—don't make a poor iOS app and put your entire energy into the watchOS app. The first experience your user will have with your apps will be the iOS app.

1. Launch Xcode. The Welcome to Xcode window will appear, as seen in Figure 1-1.

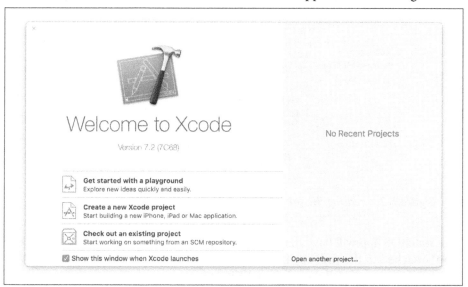

Figure 1-1. The Welcome to Xcode screen

2. Click "Create a new Xcode project." The template chooser window will appear (seen in Figure 1-2). Select "Application" in the "watchOS" section of the list, and then choose "iOS App with WatchKit App." Click Next, and on the following screen, name the project "HelloWatch." Make sure you choose Swift as the development language, and turn on "Include Notification Scene," "Include Glance Scene," and "Include Complication." Leave "Include Unit Tests" and "Include UI Tests" as they are—we won't be working with them.

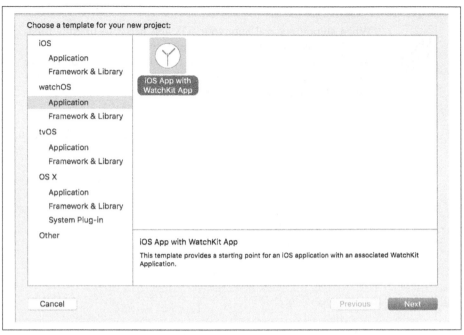

Figure 1-2. Creating the project

The watchOS app will have the same name as your main application, with "WatchKit App" attached to the end. So, if you named your iOS app "HelloWatch," the WatchKit app will be named "HelloWatch WatchKit App."

1. Open the scheme selector: it's the drop-down menu at the top-left of the Xcode window.

2. Select the HelloWatch WatchKit App scheme.

3. Build and run the app: press Command-R, and the app will build and launch in the simulator.

You'll see two windows: the phone and the watch. Both will be empty.

 When an iOS simulator is launched for the first time, it will take some time to prepare itself. This can interfere with the installation of the watchOS app. If the app doesn't appear on the simulated watch, quit both the Simulator and the Simulator (Watch) apps, and try building and running the app again.

Building for Simulator

Simulator comes with built-in support for simulating an Apple Watch. When you create an Apple Watch application and tell Xcode to build and run it, Simulator will display an additional window, in which your Apple Watch will appear (as seen in Figure 1-3).

Figure 1-3. The iOS simulator, with an Apple Watch app being simulated next to it

To run an app on the simulator, you simply select the scheme for your WatchKit application by choosing it in the lefthand side of the scheme selector, and select an iPhone simulator and Apple Watch combination in the righthand side of the scheme selector (see Figure 1-4).

Figure 1-4. Selecting an iPhone and Apple Watch simulator in the scheme selector

You can also interact with the Apple Watch simulator in much the same way as you do an actual Apple Watch. When you press Command-Shift-H, the Apple Watch will act as though you pressed the Digital Crown; when you scroll the trackpad up and down over the simulated Apple Watch screen, it will act as though you rotated the Digital Crown.

Take some time to play with the simulated Apple Watch, and get comfortable with how it works.

You can download additional simulators for use in Xcode. When you install Xcode, it includes the most recent (as at the time of download) versions of iOS and watchOS; you can also download simulators that run *older* versions of the operating system, and test your software on those.

To install these older versions, open the Xcode menu, and choose Prefences. Click the Components tab, and you'll be shown a list of simulators to download. Once they're downloaded, you can choose which version of watchOS you want to run your app through the scheme selector.

Building for the Device

To build a WatchKit application for a device, you first need to have an Apple Watch that's paired with an iPhone. When you build and install the app, you're actually building and installing an iOS app, and the watchOS app it contains is then copied to the Apple Watch.

Building and running the app on the watch is very similar to using the iOS simulator: you select the WatchKit app in the scheme selector, and choose your iPhone as the destination (see Figure 1-5). Hit Command-R to start the building and copying process, and after a moment, the various bits and pieces will be in place.

After the app has finished installing, you may or may not have to manually launch the app on your Apple Watch. If your app isn't launched immediately, you need to manually launch it by pressing once on the Digital Crown, and then locating your app's icon on the watch's home screen. Tap the app's name, and it will be launched. Xcode will attach its debugger to the watchOS app, and you can use your app.

Figure 1-5. Selecting an iPhone in the scheme selector

Congratulations! You've built an empty app. In the next chapter, we'll explore what you can do with it.

CHAPTER 2

WatchKit Apps

Put simply, a WatchKit app is an app that runs on the watch. Apps on watchOS are separate and independent binaries that run on the watch, and communicate with their parent iOS app only when they have to. This reduces latency, and ensures that the power-hungry Bluetooth radio is used as infrequently as possible.

From the user's perspective, apps on the watch are very similar to apps on the phone: they present information to the user, and respond to taps and other input. However, while the watch is an independent computer, it's incredibly underpowered compared to the iPhone. You can't do heavy processing on the watch—if you need to do hard work, you get in touch with the iPhone in the user's pocket. Additionally, certain hardware isn't best suited to being directly in contact with the user's skin at all times (for example, cellular radios), due to the fact that they emit larger amounts of energy.

It's for this reason that the Apple Watch requires the user to have an iPhone: without an iPhone providing information to the watch, the watch's utility is limited.

When you're developing an app for the Apple Watch, you'll end up building the iOS app and the watchOS app separately. These are two different targets in Xcode, but can belong to the same project. Any code or resource that needs to run on both devices needs to be added to both of the targets.

Displaying Content on the Watch

Once you have an empty WatchKit app, the next step is to show content:

1. Open the storyboard for the WatchKit app. Find *Interface.storyboard* in the *Hello-Watch WatchKitApp* folder, and open it. You'll see four interface controllers: one labeled "Interface Controller," one labeled "Glance Controller," and one labelled "Static Interface," which is connected to the final interface controller labeled

"Dynamic Interface." In this chapter, we'll be focusing on the first one, labeled "Interface Controller."

2. Add a label. If it isn't already open, open the Object Library by choosing View→Utilities→Show Object Library. Scroll down the list until you find the label, and drag it into the application's interface.

Double-click the label, and make it contain the text "Hi, Apple Watch!" When you're done, your interface should look like Figure 2-1.

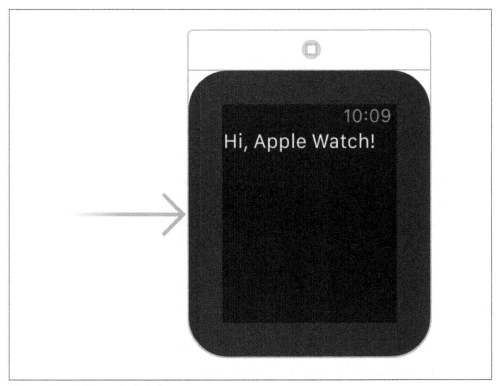

Figure 2-1. Adding the label

The way you design your interfaces on the Apple Watch is quite different than how you design interfaces on iOS. When you're designing an interface on iOS or OS X— or, indeed, most operating systems—you generally position objects wherever you like on the screen. By contrast, the layout of interfaces on the Apple Watch is *managed*: when you add items to the screen, their position and size is determined by the system, based on where they are in the list or what type of interface object they're contained in.

This also means that you can't overlap any interface objects. Objects are displayed next to each other, based on the order in which they're arranged in the Interface Builder.

When you select an object in the interface, you can configure various settings for that object in the Attributes Inspector. To bring up the Attributes Inspector, choose View→Utilities→Show Attributes Inspector.

There are two different sizes of Apple Watch: a 38mm model and a 42mm model. These two models have different screen sizes, which means that there are differing amounts of room on the screen for your interface. More content can be shown on the 42mm device than on the 38mm.

You can change the settings for different controls based on whether the watch is a 38mm or 42mm device by selecting them (clicking the + button at the left of each of the attributes in the Attributes Inspector).

When you run the app, you'll now see text on the simulated Apple Watch's screen.

Responding to Actions

Displaying stuff on the screen is good, but the real power of the Apple Watch is its ability to let users control the phone from their wrists. The most straightforward way to demonstrate this is to add a button to our "HelloWatch" app:

1. Find the Button in the Objects Library, then drag it into the interface. Place it underneath the label.

2. Open the Assistant by clicking the Assistant button at the top-right of the Xcode window—it looks like two interlinked circles (see Figure 2-2).

Figure 2-2. The Assistant button at the top-right of the Xcode window opens the Assistant editor

3. Open *InterfaceController.swift* in the Assistant by clicking the leftmost element in the Jump Bar at the top of the assistant, selecting Automatic, and then choosing "InterfaceController.swift" (see Figure 2-3).

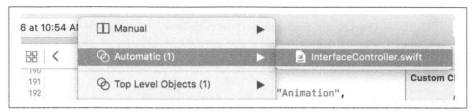

Figure 2-3. The Jump Bar, selecting the InterfaceController.swift file

This object is in charge of providing the content for this *page* in the WatchKit app.

4. Connect the button to the code by holding down the Control key on the keyboard and drag the button into the `InterfaceController` class. A pop-up window will appear, allowing you to define a connection between the interface and the code (see Figure 2-4). Set the connection type to "Action" and name it "buttonTapped." Click Connect, and a new method called `buttonTapped` will be added to your code.

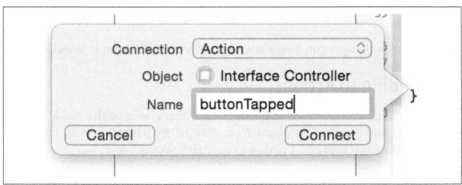

Figure 2-4. Creating the interface

An *action* is a method that's run when the user interacts with the interface. For example, when the user taps a button, slides a slider, or otherwise does anything to the interface, you can hook up an action method to run in response.

The other type of connection is called an *outlet*. An outlet is a variable that is connected to the object in your interface at runtime, allowing your code to interact with the contents of your interface.

Create an outlet for the label by control-dragging from the label into the `Interface Controller` class; when the connection dialog box appears, set the connection type to "Outlet," and name it "label."

What we'll do now is make the label change its text when the button is tapped. Add the code to the `buttonTapped` method:

```
@IBAction func buttonTapped() {
    label.setText("Hi Hello Hi")
}
```

Test it out by running the app, tap the button, and see it change.

Controls

When you're designing a WatchKit app, you have quite a few tools to work with. If you scroll through the list of objects available in the Object Library, you'll see a large collection of different elements, which you can drag into your interface and let the user interact with.

The only way you can add objects to your interfaces in WatchKit is through the Interface Builder. Unlike when programming for iOS, you can't create them at runtime using code. The only way to work with interface objects is through outlets.

Additionally, your code never retrieves data from controls. You'll notice that there are setter methods like `setText` for labels, but no getter methods like `text`.

In WatchKit, a "page" of content is managed by an *interface controller*. To create an interface controller, you subclass the `WKInterfaceController` class, and add your actions and outlets for that chunk of content in your WatchKit app.

There are some important methods that your `WKInterfaceController` subclass should implement.

- `awakeWithContext` is called when the interface controller is loaded from disk. In this method, you prepare your interface objects, and give them their initial values.

- `willActivate` is called when the interface controller is about to be shown to the user.

- `didDeactivate` is called when the interface controller is no longer visible to the user.

In fact, these methods are so important that the *InterfaceController.swift* file that Xcode generates for you when you create a new project already includes them:

```
override func awakeWithContext(context: AnyObject?) {
    super.awakeWithContext(context)

    // Configure interface objects here.
}
```

```
override func willActivate() {
    // This method is called when watch view controller is about to
    // be visible to user
    super.willActivate()
}

override func didDeactivate() {
    // This method is called when watch view controller is no longer visible
    super.didDeactivate()
}
```

Once you know your way around interface controllers, it's helpful to know about the four most useful controls available to you: labels, image views, table views, and menus.

Text and Labels

When you want to show text to to the user, you most often use a *label*. Labels in WatchKit are instances of the `WKInterfaceLabel` class.

Labels in WatchKit can display either *plain text* or *attributed text*. Attributed text is text that contains style information throughout the text, like making certain characters bold.

To update the text shown in a `WKInterfaceLabel`, you use the `setText` method:

```
label.setText("Hi Hello Hi")
```

To show attributed text using an `NSAttributedString`, use the `setAttributedText` method. You can also set the color of a label using `setTextColor`.

Automatically Updating labels

Some labels that appear on the screen need to be updated frequently, and it's not especially convenient to have to perform these changes yourself.

One of the most common cases where you'd need to perform frequent updates is the case of a label that shows the current time, or shows a countdown timer. Fortunately, there are two special subclasses of `WKInterfaceLabel` that handle these specific situations.

- `WKInterfaceDate` is a special label that shows the current time and date.
- `WKInterfaceTimer` is a special label that counts down to a date. When you call `setDate` on this label, the label automatically begins counting down toward this date (if the date is in the future), or counting upwards from that date (if the date is in the past or is right now).

`WKInterfaceTimer` is a display-only object. When the label is counting down toward a specific date, it won't notify you when that date is reached. If you want to be notified when this happens, you need to set up your own `NSTimer` object.

Images

To display images on your watch, you use the `WKInterfaceImage` class. This object displays both static and animated images.

There are several methods you can use to display an image on a `WKInterfaceImage`:

- `setImage` takes a `UIImage` object and displays it.
- `setImageData` takes an `NSData` object that contains an image. It loads the image into a `UIImage` and displays it.
- `setImageNamed` makes the watch look for an image with the specified name, and displays it. If it can't be found, the image view shows no image.

You can always clear the image from an image view by calling `setImage` and passing `nil`.

`WKInterfaceImage` supports the same image formats as iOS. However, it's better if you use PNG and JPEG images, as these don't need to be converted by iOS before being sent to the watch.

If you send an image that's too big for the control, it's scaled down so that it fits in the control (preserving the image's aspect ratio).

Finally, images can be given a tint color using `setTintColor`. This allows you to save space by providing a single grayscale image, which is then filled with a color. Because this tinting is done on the watch, you can update the color of a `WKInterfaceImage` at any time, and without having to transfer an entirely new `UIImage` to the watch.

Animations

In addition to showing single images, you can also use a `WKInterfaceImage` to display animations. You can either configure a `WKInterfaceImage` to show an animated image using the Interface Builder, or you can do it with code.

To create an animated image, you first need to have all of the frames of your image ready, and add them to your application. You do this in the same way you add static images: by dragging and dropping them into an asset bundle. The key difference between static and animated images is that the frames attached to each animated image must all have the same name, suffixed with an increasing number.

For example, if you want an animation named "Animation," you'd add an image called "Animation0," a second called "Animation1," and so on (see Figure 2-5). You can have up to 1024 frames in an animation.

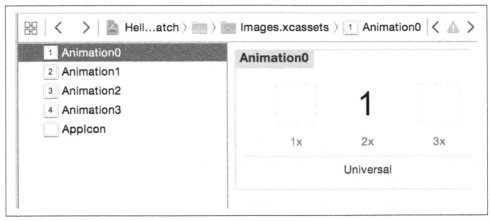

Figure 2-5. Creating frame images for an animation

To set up an animated image in the Interface Builder, you set the name of the image to "Animation" (or whatever the name of your animation is)—*without* the frame number suffix. Next, change Animate from "No" to "Yes," and specify how long the animation should run in seconds (see Figure 2-6: in this case, each loop of the animation will take one second). The Interface Builder won't recognize the image, so you won't see a preview in the window, but when you run the app, it'll work fine.

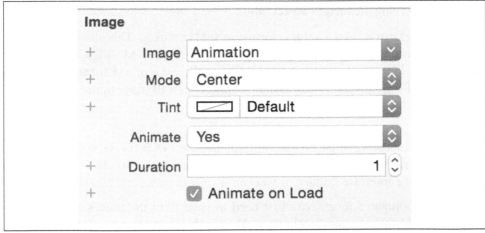

Figure 2-6. Setting up an animation in the Interface Builder

Alternatively, you can set up an animation in code. The way that you interact with the WKInterfaceImage actually remains the same: you simply provide it with a UIImage object by calling the setImage or setImageNamed methods.

The difference is in how the UIImage object is set up. To create an *animated* UIImage, you use the animatedImageNamed method, and provide the name and duration of your animation:

```
let animatedImage =
    UIImage.animatedImageNamed("Animation",
                                duration: 1.0)

self.imageView.setImage(animatedImage)
```

Menus

A *menu* is a place where you can put additional actions that the user can perform. These actions aren't visible until the user pushes on the screen with a little extra force (a *force touch*). When the user does this, and the interface controller that's currently active has a menu, menu items appear. You can see an example of a menu in Figure 2-7.

Figure 2-7. A menu, with a single menu item

Menus are used all over the Apple Watch to provide access to extra actions that aren't critical to the main functionality of whatever you're using. For example, when you force-touch the notifications list, a menu appears that contains a single menu item, which lets you dismiss all notifications at once.

Menus don't include a button to close them. To close them, you tap anywhere outside the menu's buttons, or you press the Digital Crown.

Menus are attached to interface controllers. To add a menu, you drag and drop the Menu item from the Object Library onto an interface controller.

Unlike the other controls, you don't work with code to configure menus. In fact, you don't really configure menus at all—you can't customize their appearance in code, and you can't change any properties at runtime. The only thing you can do is add them to your interface, and connect the buttons to methods in your interface controller's code.

Each menu contains between one and four menu items. Menu items themselves contain an image and a label. You can select from a list of different built-in images, or you can add a custom image to your app's asset catalog.

Menu items need to have both an image and a label. If the text for the label is empty, or if the custom image that you provide can't be found, the menu item won't appear.

While a menu can contain up to four items, it's a good idea to try to keep this number as close to one as possible. The more items you add, the smaller they all get. When you're on a device that the user will be looking at for only a few seconds at a time, anything that reduces readability is a bad thing.

Where possible, try to avoid using menus entirely, as they're not immediately visible to the user—remember, users have to force-touch to see if there's anything there at all, and they may not think to try doing it.

You connect the button to the interface controller by following the same steps outlined for a `WKInterfaceButton`: control-drag from the item in the outline pane into your `WKInterfaceController` class and create an action; this action is called when the button is tapped.

To test menus in the iOS simulator, you need to indicate that you want to simulate a force touch. To do this, follow these steps:

1. Open the Hardware menu, and choose Force Touch Pressure→Deep Press.

2. Click on the screen, and the watch will react as if you'd pressed hard on it.

3. Choose Hardware→Force Touch Pressure→Shallow Press to go back to regular presses.

 You can also change the force touch pressure with the Command-Shift-1 and Command-Shift-2 keyboard shortcuts.

Tables

A table is a list of content that the user can scroll through. Tables are represented by the WKInterfaceTable class.

Tables in WatchKit work a little differently to their equivalents in iOS. In iOS, table views call back to a controller object to ask questions about how many rows there are in the list, and, for each cell, what content should be displayed. This kind of interaction would generate way too much back-and-forth traffic for the Apple Watch, which means that WKInterfaceTables are optimized to support preparing the entire content of the list all at once.

The way that it works is as follows: at design time, you define a number of row types. For each type of row, you lay out the controls that go in the row. You also give the row type an *identifier*, which is a string, plus the name of a *row controller* class that will store outlets to the controls that go in the cell.

At runtime, you tell the WKInterfaceTable about the number of cells that are in the table, and what the row type is. Doing this creates instances of all of the row controller classes. You can then ask the table for a specific row controller, and use that object's outlets to access the controls in a specific label.

 Unlike in iOS, cells in a WatchKit table are empty by default. You'll need to add controls to them yourself, and add outlets for each control that you add to the row's controller class.

For example, let's say you want to add a table that displays a list of words. This will mean that each cell will need a label, and you'll need a way of sending the correct word to each cell's label.

To do this, follow these steps:

1. Drag a table from the Objects inspector into your interface.

2. In one of your source code files, create a class called MyRow. Make it a subclass of NSObject. (You can create a new file for this class, or you can add the class to an existing *.swift* file.)

3. By default, tables come with a single row controller already set up. Select the row controller in the outline—it has a yellow circular icon—and set its Identifier to MyRow in the Attributes Inspector. Then go to the Identity Inspector, and set its Class to MyRow.

4. Set up the row by dragging a label into the row's interface. Then, open the MyRow class in the Assistant, hold down the control key, and drag from the label into the MyRow class. Create a new outlet for the label called label.

5. In your interface controller's awakeWithContext method, add the following code:

```
// An array of strings to show in the table
let dataToDisplay = ["Hello", "World", "This", "Is", "A", "Table"]

myTable.setNumberOfRows(dataToDisplay.count, withRowType: "MyRow")

for i in 0 ..< dataToDisplay.count {
    let rowController = myTable.rowControllerAtIndex(i) as? MyRow

    rowController?.label.setText(dataToDisplay[i])
}
```

6. Finally, run the application; you'll see a scrollable list of words.

In addition to simply creating rows using the setNumberOfRows method, you can also use the insertRowsAtIndexes(_, withRow Type:) and removeRowsAtIndexes methods to add and remove rows.

Picker Views

A *picker view* displays a collection of options that the user can select from, by either swiping the screen or rotating the Digital Crown. Picker views can display text and images in a variety of ways; they can display a rotating list of captions, a stack of images, or a sequence of images.

Picker views are configured by creating a collection of WKPickerItem objects, which you provide to a WKInterfacePicker object.

To add a picker item, you drag a Picker from the Object Library into your interface controller. To provide the picker with content, you connect it to an outlet in your interface controller's class, and call setItems to give it the list of WKPickerItems it should show.

For example, let's say `self.picker` is a variable that refers to a `WKPickerView`. In this case, you could make it show the strings "Item 0," "Item 1," and "Item 2" in it by doing this:

```
var listContent : [WKPickerItem] = []

for i in 0...2 {
    let item = WKPickerItem()
    item.title = "Item \(i)"
    listContent.append(item);
}

self.picker.setItems(listContent)
```

Picker items can contain images, text, or a combination of both. The specifics of what's shown depend on the list's style.

As the user interacts with the picker, the picker calls whichever method is connected in the interface builder, much like a button does when the user taps on it. This method receives an `Int`, representing the index of the currently selected item. The first item is given the index 0, the second item is given the index 1, and so on.

 The `WKInterfacePicker` doesn't provide a way to *retrieve* the `WKPickerItems` that you've provided to it. You need to keep track of those yourself.

```
@IBAction func pickerSelectedItem(value: Int) {
    print ("Picker selected item \(value)")
}
```

 You can also link animated images with the picker, so that the animation is at the first frame when the picker has selected the first item, and at the last frame when picker is at the last item. To do this, you provide the picker view with an animation, by using the `WKInterfacePicker`'s `setCoordinatedImages` method. This method takes an array of `WKInterfaceImages`, which are animated as the picker rotates. To learn more about presenting an animated image, see "Animations" on page 17.

Playing Media

In addition to showing text and images, the Apple Watch can also play back video and audio. This is done through a *media player interface controller*, which you present from your interface controller.

Presenting any kind of media means loading it from a file. This means that if you want to play sound or video, the file that contains that content needs to be on the watch. The most straightforward way to do this is to embed the file in the application by following these steps:

1. Locate the video or audio file on your computer that you want to play in the Apple Watch app.

2. Drag it into the Project Navigator, at the lefthand side of the Xcode window.

3. Xcode will ask you which targets the file should be added to—that is, should it be added to the iOS app, the watchOS app, or both? You can see the window in Figure 2-8.

4. Add the project to the WatchKit app. The file will then be copied to the watch when the app is installed.

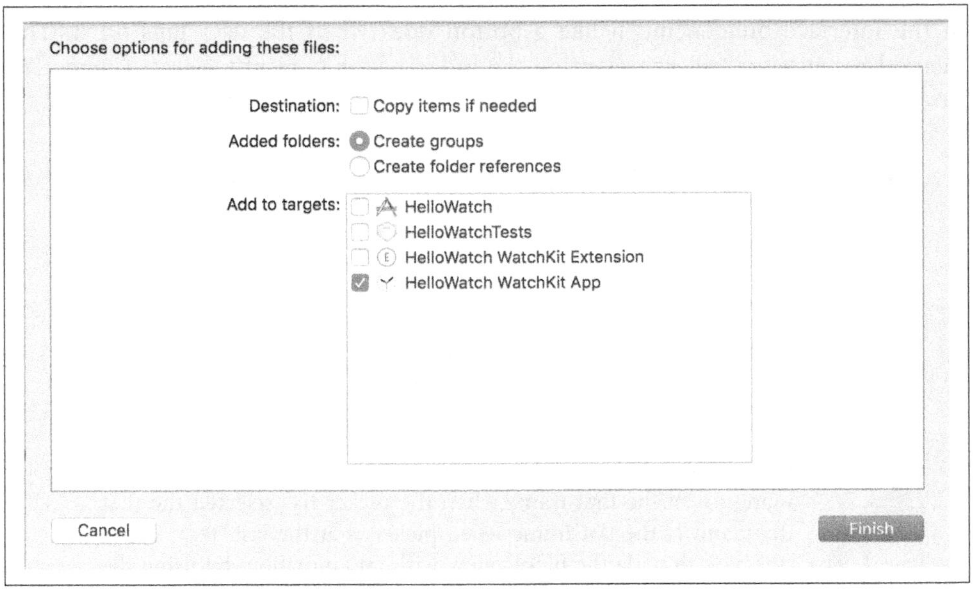

Figure 2-8. Adding a file to the project

To access a file that's embedded in this way, you use the NSBundle class to get the location of the file within the watch. For example, if you've got a video file called *Video.m4v* included as part of the application's resources, you can determine its URL like so:

```
guard let videoFileURL = NSBundle.mainBundle()
    .URLForResource("Video", withExtension: "m4v") else {

    print("Couldn't find the video!")
```

```
    return
}
```

In this example, we've wrapped it in a `guard` statement. This means that if the file *cannot* be found, the code will log an error message and bail out. Doing this means that if we get past the `guard` statement, the `videoFileURL` variable is guaranteed to have a value you can use.

Once you have the location of a video file, you can present it using a media player:

```
self.presentMediaPlayerControllerWithURL(videoFileURL, options: nil) {
    (didPlayToEnd, endTime, error) in

    print("Video player ended; played to end = \(didPlayToEnd), " +
        "end time = \(endTime), error = \(error)")

}
```

When you call `presentMediaPlayerControllerWithURL`, you provide the URL of the file that you want to play, and a dictionary containing additional information on *how* it should be played, and a closure to run when the controller disappears. The video will then appear, allowing the user to view it.

When the user is done playing the video, the closure is called, and receives three parameters: a `Bool` value indicating whether the video was played through to the end, an `NSTimeInterval` value representing where in the video the user was when the video was closed, and an optional `NSError` object that describes any problem that was encountered while playing the video.

You can also use a media player controller to play audio, without video.

The `options` parameter lets you control how the user interacts with the media being presented. For example, if you wanted to make the video automatically play, you'd prepare a dictionary containing the `WKMediaPlayerControllerOptionsAutoplayKey` key set to `true`:

```
let options = [
    WKMediaPlayerControllerOptionsAutoplayKey: true
]

self.presentMediaPlayerControllerWithURL(videoFileURL, options: options) {
    (didPlayToEnd, endTime, error) in
```

```
        print("Video player ended; played to end = \(didPlayToEnd), " +
            "end time = \(endTime), error = \(error)")

    }
```

Using this dictionary, you can set things like whether the content loops, how video should be scaled to fit in the available space, and at what time the media starts playing. For the full list of available options, see the section "Media Player Options" in the `WKInterfaceController` documentation (*http://bit.ly/media-options*).

Getting Text from the User

In a lot of apps, you'll often want to get some kind of text from the user. The Apple Watch is way too small to fit a keyboard on the screen, which means that there are only a couple of ways for the watch to get text input from the user.

The first method is to provide a list of predefined choices, and let the user select one. The second method is to let users speak to the device, and get their speech transcribed into text.

WatchKit combines both of these methods into one tool, called the *text input controller*. The text input controller displays a list of options, which your app determines, as well as letting the user choose an emoji image or use the Apple Watch's built-in microphone to dictate a reply.

To present the text input controller, you call the method `presentTextInputControllerWithSuggestions(_, allowedInputMode: completion:)`, which takes three parameters:

- The first parameter is an array of strings, each of which is an option that the user can select. This array is optional.

- The second parameter allows you to choose whether the user can provide only plain text, choose emoji images, or choose animated emoji images. You generally want to provide users with as much room to express themselves as you can, so limit their options for replying only after you've thought about it a great deal.

- The third parameter is a closure that's called by the system after the user has finished with the text input controller. This closure takes a single parameter, which is an array of `NSObjects`. This array contains one or more strings and `NSData` objects—strings are selected options or the results of dictation, whereas `NSData` objects are images, which can be decoded using the `UIImage` class's `UIImage(data:)` method. This array can also be empty, which indicates that the user chose to cancel entering text.

You can also call `dismissTextInputController` to get rid of the text input controller, if you decide you don't need it anymore. Be careful about calling this, though; if the user is in the middle of dictating something, and the input controller goes away, then you risk annoying her.

If you want to try presenting a text input controller, add the following method to a button's action method (see "Responding to Actions" on page 13):

```
let suggestions = ["Yes", "No", "I guess?", "Huh?"]

self.presentTextInputControllerWithSuggestions(
    suggestions, allowedInputMode: .Plain) { (results : [AnyObject]?) in

        guard let theResults = results else {
            print ("No text provided")
            return
        }

        for result in theResults {
            print ("Result: \(result)")
        }
}
```

 Dictation and emoji aren't supported by the WatchKit simulator. You'll need to use a real device to test them out.

Working with Multiple Interface Controllers

Often, a WatchKit app will only need a single screen's worth of content. However, as an app gets more complex, you won't want to try to fit everything into one location, and you'll need to put some controls and information on other screens.

There are two ways that users of the Apple Watch interact with screens of content in apps:

Hierarchical navigation
This works similarly to the way `UINavigationControllers` do in iOS: when you want to show new content, you push a new screen, which slides in from the right-hand side. When users want to go back, they tap the Back arrow at the top left of the watch display.

Page-based navigation
This works in a similar way to the home screen on an iPhone or iPad, in that the user can swipe left and right to see different pages of content.

Hierarchical navigation works best when you need to let the user drill down into a specific piece of information. For example, a news app could show a list of topics, and tapping on each topic would push a screen containing the relevant headlines.

Page-based navigation is good for situations where you have different screens of content that don't necessarily need to connect to each other. For example, an app that displays the locations of the user's friends could show a screen for each friend in a page-based way, allowing the user to swipe left and right to see each friend.

Your application can use hierarchical navigation or page-based navigation. You can't use both in the same app, because both of these styles of navigation rely on left-right animations to change the screen's content. When you push a new screen of content in an app that uses hierarchical navigation, the new screen slides in from the right; however, when you move from one screen to the next, the new screen would also slide in from the right. To avoid confusion, you can't mix and match.

Regardless of whether your app uses hierarchical or page-based navigation, the interface controllers that contain each screen's worth of content need to be connected. There are two main ways you can do this: you can connect the interface controllers in the interface builder using *segues*, or you can give each interface controller a name and manually summon it into existence in your code.

To create a segue, you hold down the Control button and drag from one object to another. Only certain objects can be connected via a segue:

- Interface controllers can connect to other interface controllers via a "next page" segue.
- Buttons, groups and table rows can connect to other interface controllers via either "push" or "modal" segues. Once you release the mouse button, you'll be asked what kind of segue you want.

Hierarchical Navigation

To set up a hierarchical navigation in your app, you create a "push" segue that links a button to another interface controller. When you tap on this object, the second interface controller will appear, and the user can go back by tapping on the back arrow.

If you want to try this out for yourself, follow these steps:

1. Add a button to your interface controller, and add a new interface controller that you want to show when the button is tapped.
2. Hold down the Control key, then click and drag from the button to the interface controller.

3. A list of segue types will appear; click Push. This will create the segue that links the button to the interface controller.

4. Run the app. When you tap the button, the interface controller will appear.

If you don't want to use segues to connect screens, you can also create a hierarchical navigation structure in code. To do this, follow these steps:

1. Select the interface controller that you want to navigate to, and go to the Identity inspector.

2. Set the interface controller's Identifier to something useful—for example, `detailScreen`.

3. In order to present this interface controller, call the `pushControllerWithName(_, context:)` method:

```
self.pushControllerWithName("secondScreen", context: nil)
```

You can also return the user to the previous screen by calling `popController`, and return the user to the very beginning by calling `popToRootController`.

Page-Based Navigation

The alternative to hierarchy-based navigation in a watchOS app is page-based navigation. In page-based navigation, the watch shows a horizontally scrolling list of interface controllers, and you swipe left and right to access them. This is very similar in terms of design to how the home screen on an iPhone works.

To create a page-based navigation flow for your application, you need to include a "next page" segue between your interface controllers. You can do this by following these steps:

1. Hold down the Control key, and drag from the interface controller that you'd like to appear first in the list to another.

2. A menu containing possible segues will appear. Select "next page" in the menu that appears.

3. Run the app. When you swipe from right to left, the second interface controller will appear.

When the app starts up, the Apple Watch uses this chain of segues to build a horizontally scrolling collection, with the first view controller at the far left, and each interface controller connected via a "next page" segue on the right. Each screen can be scrolled vertically, based on the content that's stored inside it, and if the user scrolls horizontally, he's taken to the additional screens.

You can connect a chain of interface controllers like this, by linking the first screen to the second, the second to the third, and so on.

When you want to create "next page" segues, you need to connect the two interface controllers themselves, and not any object that's stored inside the interface controllers. Don't drag from inside the interface controller, because when you do that, you aren't dragging from the controller itself.

When using page-based navigation, you typically won't often need to change the pages. If you *do* want to do this, then use the Identity Inspector to give each interface controller a name, and then call `WKInterfaceController.reloadRootControllers WithNames(_,contexts:)`. This method takes an array of interface controller names and replaces the collection of pages with new interface controllers:

```
WKInterfaceController.reloadRootControllersWithNames(["mainScreen",
    "additionalScreen"], contexts: nil)
```

Don't call `reloadRootControllersWithNames` after the user has started using the application. Changing the way that the interface is laid out after users have gotten used to how things work is confusing, and will put them off using your app.

Instead, call `reloadRootControllersWithNames` at application launch time—for example, in the `init` or `awakeWithContext` methods of your interface controllers.

Modal Presentation

The last way to let your users get access to other screens is via a *modal* presentation. When you use a modal presentation to show an interface controller, the interface controller takes over the entire screen.

You use a modal presentation when you need to interrupt the user's experience. For example, if the user is in the middle of some task, like requesting an Uber, you could present a modal interface controller to let her know that her driver was nearby.

It's important to avoid interrupting the users' experience with alert screens as much as possible. Your users will only have a few seconds at a time to interact with your Watch Kit app, and slowing them down by popping up a modal alert box will only annoy them.

You can use either segues or code to present an interface controller modally. To use a segue, connect a button, group, or table row to an interface controller, and then create a "modal" segue. To modally present an interface controller using code, give the interface controller an identifier in the interface builder's Identity inspector, and then call presentControllerWithName(_, context:):

```
self.presentControllerWithName("detailScreen", context: nil)
```

 You can also present a page-based layout modally, either with segues or with code.

To do this using segues, connect the screens that should be linked together in a page-based navigation screen using the "next page" segue, just as usual. Then, create a "modal" segue that connects the screen you want to present the screen from to the first screen that should appear.

If you'd prefer to show a page-based layout using code, call present ControllerWithNames(_, contexts:), and pass in the array of names of interface controllers.

If you simply need to present an alert (such as some text), you can also use the method presentAlertControllerWithTitle(_, message:, preferredStyle:, actions:). This method modally presents an interface controller containing a title and message, along with a number of buttons.

To show an alert, you first prepare the buttons you want it to have. You do this by creating an array of WKAlertAction objects, which each contain two things—the text that the button should display and a closure that should be run if the user taps the button:

```
let actions = [
    WKAlertAction(title: "OK", style: WKAlertActionStyle.Default, handler: {
        print("OK button tapped")
    })
]
```

 All alerts must have at least one button.

Once you have the list of actions you want to attach to the alert, you simply need to call presentAlertControllerWithTitle, and provide the title and optional message, as well as the list of actions and the layout that the alert should have:

```
let alertTitle = "Error!"
let alertMessage = "There was a problem!"
```

```
self.presentAlertControllerWithTitle(alertTitle,
                              message: alertMessage,
                              preferredStyle: .Alert,
                              actions: actions)
```

Communicating with the Device

The Apple Watch is a separate computer from the iPhone. However, to access the wider world, your watchOS app will need to communicate with its counterpart iOS app. To achieve this, you use a separate framework called *WatchConnectivity*.

This framework is available on both iOS and watchOS, and is the mechanism for sending information to and from the other device. You use the same API on both devices, which simplifies the work you need to do.

To start using WatchConnectivity, you `import` the framework as follows:

```
import WatchConnectivity
```

All of your interaction with the other device is mediated through a `WCSession` object. You don't construct this object yourself; instead, you ask for the default session:

```
let session = WCSession.defaultSession()
```

Additionally, to work with the session, you need to provide it with an object that conforms to the `WCSessionDelegate` method. One way to do this is by creating an extension that makes your interface controller conform to the protocol, like so:

```
extension InterfaceController : WCSessionDelegate {

    @available(watchOSApplicationExtension 2.2, *)
    func session(session: WCSession, activationDidCompleteWithState
        activationState: WCSessionActivationState, error: NSError?) {

        print("Session activated!")
    }

    func sessionDidDeactivate(session: WCSession) {
        print("Session deactivated!")

    }

    func sessionDidBecomeInactive(session: WCSession) {
        print("Session became inactive!")
    }

    func sessionReachabilityDidChange(session: WCSession) {
        print("Reachability changed to \(session.reachable)")

    }

}
```

Note the @available tag on session(_, activationDidComplete WithState: , error:). This exists to mark that the method is only part of the protocol in watchOS 2.2 and later.

When you have an object that conforms to the WCSessionDelegate, you can provide it to the WCSession as its delegate. In this example, self is an instance of Interface Controller:

```
session.delegate = self
```

A session does nothing until it's activated. To activate it, use the activateSession method:

```
session.activateSession()
```

This call to activateSession is asynchronous: it can take a moment for the session to become active. When it does, the activationDidCompleteWithState method in WCSessionDelegate is called.

In addition to a session being active or not, the counterpart app may or may not be *reachable*. For example, you might activate a WCSession, and then go for a run with your watch, leaving your phone behind. The session remains active, but the phone is no longer reachable from the watch. This means that before you attempt to send any message to the other device, you need to ensure that the reachable property is true.

An iPhone can be paired with multiple watches, but only one session is active at a time between the phone and a watch.

Sending and Receiving Messages

The most straightforward way to send data from the watch to the phone, or from the phone to the watch, is by sending *messages*. A message is a dictionary that contains simple data: strings, numbers, dates, NSData objects, or arrays or dictionaries containing these types.

To send a message, you first construct the dictionary that represents the message you want to deliver. The message can be anything you like. For example:

```
let message = [
    "message":"hi"
]
```

Once you have your message, you send it, using the sendMessage method on your WCSession:

```
WCSession.defaultSession().sendMessage(message,
                                    replyHandler: nil,
                                    errorHandler: { (error) in

    print("Got an error sending to the phone: \(error)")
})
```

The `sendMessage` method takes three parameters: the message itself, a reply handler closure (more on that in a moment!), and a closure that's called if there was an error sending the message to the other device.

When this is called, the message is transmitted over the radio link to the counterpart app; when the message is received, the counterpart `WCSession`'s delegate receives the `session(_, didReceiveMessage:)` method call:

```
func session(session: WCSession,
    didReceiveMessage message: [String : AnyObject]) {
    print("Phone received message: \(message)")
}
```

Sometimes, a message needs a reply. For example, your watchOS app may need to ask the iOS app for a list of strings to display; the iOS app will receive the request, and will then need to reply to that request.

To enable this, you provide a closure for the `replyHandler` parameter when calling `sendMessage`:

```
WCSession.defaultSession().sendMessage(message,
                                    replyHandler: { (replyMessage) in
    print("Got a reply from the phone: \(replyMessage)")
}, errorHandler: { (error) in
    print("Got an error sending to the phone: \(error)")
})
```

The `replyHandle` takes a single parameter: a dictionary, containing the reply sent by the counterpart app. It's up to you to interpret the contents of this dictionary.

When you send a message and provide a `replyHandler`, the counterpart app's session delegate receives a slightly different method call: `session(_, didReceiveMessage:, replyHandler:)`.

This method works identically, receiving the message sent from the other device; it *also* receives a `replyHandler` closure, which it is required to call before the method returns. When you call this closure, you provide the dictionary that you'd like to reply with:

```
func session(session: WCSession,
    didReceiveMessage message: [String : AnyObject],
    replyHandler: ([String : AnyObject]) -> Void) {

    print("Phone received message that needs a reply: \(message)")
```

```
let replyMessage = [
    "reply":"hello!"
]

replyHandler(replyMessage)

}
```

 You must call the `replyHandler` before the method ends. If you don't, your app will crash.

Moving Between Devices Using Handoff

Handoff is a technology that's built into iOS, OS X, and watchOS, which allows the user to begin an activity on one of their devices and continue it on another.

For example, if you're writing an email on your iPhone, your Mac is made aware of this fact, and displays an icon in the Dock. If you click on that icon in the Dock, the Mail application on OS X launches, and shows the draft email that you were just editing. You can then finish writing the email on your Mac, and send it from there.

Handoff works in both directions—you can start an activity on your Mac and finish it on your iPhone. It also supports handing off an activity between devices of the same type—for example, you can hand off from an iPhone to an iPad.

Handoff also works on the Apple Watch, and it's a powerful technology that allows you to let users start doing something on the watch, and continue it on any of their other devices.

Before you start adding support for handoff to your applications, it's worth taking a moment to think about what activities users might want to continue from one device to another. In the case of mail, it's likely that users might want to continue reading or writing a specific message, but they probably won't care about synchronizing where in the list of messages they are. Don't forget that when you tell the system about an activity that the user is performing, an icon will appear on her iOS device's lock screen and in her Mac's dock. This can get a little annoying, so it pays to think about what's important and what's not.

Handoff works through the `NSUserActivity` class. A *user activity* contains two critical pieces of information: a string that identifies the *type* of the activity and a dictionary containing the *context* of the activity:

- The type of the activity is a period-separated string, like *com.oreilly.CoolWatch-App.chatting*. The activity type needs to have your iOS application's bundle identifier as its prefix (which, in this example, would be *com.oreilly.CoolWatchApp*).

- The context of the activity is a dictionary containing additional information that describes details of what the user is doing. To continue our example, the context dictionary might contain information like the username of the person the user is chatting to.

To support *receiving* an activity that's being handed off by another device, you need to add some information to your iOS app's *Info.plist* file. This file provides information about an app (for example, its name and icon) to the rest of iOS.

To add support for a handoff activity, you first work out what you want to call the activity. Earlier, we used *com.oreilly.CoolWatchApp.chatting*; again, the type identifier can be anything you like, as long as it begins with your app's bundle identifier. The activity's type identifier is never shown to the user, and is only used in your code.

Once you've figured out the activity type string, you create an array inside the iOS app's *Info.plist* file called `NSUserActivityTypes`, and add your activity type to that array (see Figure 2-9.)

Key	Type	Value
88 〈 〉 HelloWatch 〉 HelloWatch 〉 Supporting Files 〉 Info.plist 〉 No Selection		
▼ Information Property List	Dictionary	(15 items)
▼ NSUserActivityTypes	Array	(1 item)
Item 0	String	au.com.secretlab.SwiftDevForAppleWatch.funActivity
Bundle versions string, short	String	1.0
Bundle version	String	1
Bundle identifier	String	au.com.secretlab.SwiftDevForAppleWatch.$(PRODUCT_NAME:rfc1034identifier)

Figure 2-9. Setting up an activity type

Once this has been added to your iOS app's *Info.plist* file, the iOS app has declared that it's capable of *receiving* that type of activity from other devices. To *share* that activity, you use the `NSUserActivity` class to indicate what the user is doing.

To do this, you call `updateUserActivity(_, userInfo:, webpageURL:)` and pass in the activity type and context dictionary, as in the following code:

```
// Define the activity that the user is doing
let activityType = "au.com.secretlab.SwiftDevForAppleWatch.funActivity"

// Add some additonal information that provides more context
let activityInfo = [
    "additionalInfoForTheApp": "tennis"
]

// Indicate to the system that the user
```

```
// is now doing an activity
self.updateUserActivity(activityType, userInfo: activityInfo, webpageURL: nil)
```

 You can also optionally pass in an NSURL object that contains the URL of a web page to load the activity in a browser; however, we'll be focusing on using handoff with apps in this book.

When you call updateUserActivity, all other nearby devices that belong to the user *and* have an app installed that's capable of handling that type of activity are notified that the user is currently performing an activity; as a result, the application's icon is shown on the iOS lock screen, and in the OS X Dock. When the user swipes up on the icon in the iOS lock screen, or clicks on the app in the Dock, the application is activated, and its application delegate object receives the application(_, continueUserActivity:, restorationHandler:) method:

```
func application(application: UIApplication,
    continueUserActivity userActivity: NSUserActivity,
              restorationHandler: ([AnyObject]?) -> Void) -> Bool {

    print("Handling activity \(userActivity.activityType) " +
        "(parameters: \(userActivity.userInfo)")
    return true
}
```

This method receives three parameters: the UIApplication or NSApplication object that represents the current app, the NSUserActivity object that was prepared on the other device, and a closure that should be called if your application created any view controllers or windows as a result of resuming the activity (for example, if you opened a chat window to continue the user's conversation, you pass in that window to the closure).

Using handoffs, you can let your user quickly and easily move between devices with a minimum of effort. Add this feature, and your users will thank you.

Wrapping Up

In this chapter, we've introduced a number of fundamental watchOS elements. Interface controllers contain the content that your users will see and interact with, including the many different types of controls; additionally, interface controllers can be linked together to create more complex applications.

In the next chapter, we'll look at a more specialized type of interface seen in watchOS: *glances*.

CHAPTER 3

Glances

The iPhone is usually stashed away (either in a bag or pocket), and because it's not a wearable device, it's not always within easy reach. With the Apple Watch, however, users are able to find out information by simply looking at their wrists: your app can show a screen that users can look at quickly. This screen is called a *glance*.

Glances show supplemental information that is related to the content that your app provides. Not all apps need to have a glance, but having a screen of content that shows just the most important information that your user cares about can be a tremendous benefit.

In this chapter, you'll learn what glances are used for, how to design a glance, and how to add a glance to your WatchKit application.

Working with Glances

A glance is just a single screen of content. Glances do not show any scrolling content, which means that you need to be very considerate of the most important information your user will care about; for example, if you're making a news application for the watch, you won't be able to fit the entire content of a news article, or even multiple headlines. Instead, you'll have to select the single most important headline that the user is likely to care about, and display only that.

Apps only get a single glance screen. You can't create more than one screen, because it's being shown alongside the glances from all of the *other* apps that the user has on his watch.

It's important to show information very clearly. The user is going to be looking at your glance while they're on the run, and won't have time to read more than a couple of words. Don't try to pack the screen full of text; instead, try to reduce your information down to numbers, symbols, pictures, or just one or two words.

Another important constraint placed upon glances is that they're for display only. No interactive content is allowed, and if the user taps on the glance, the watch launches the main app. Again, this is because glances are designed for quickly showing a small amount of highly important information; if a user wants to do something more in-depth, she'll use the WatchKit app. (And if she wants to do something even more in-depth than what the WatchKit app allows, she'll pull out her iPhone and use that instead.)

Creating a Glance

To create a glance, you create an interface controller and designate it as the glance interface. You do this by locating the glance interface controller in the objects library and dragging it into the interface (Figure 3-1). (The glance interface controller is actually just a normal interface controller, but Xcode will treat it slightly differently because of how it's going to be used.)

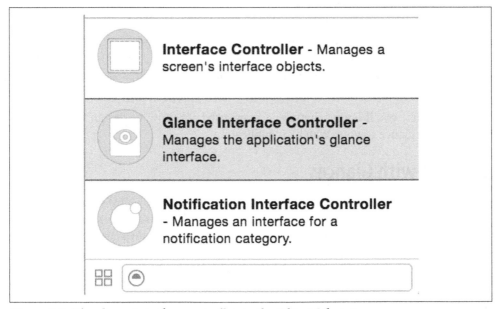

Figure 3-1. The glance interface controller, in the Object Library

 If you chose to create a glance when creating the project, as we suggested you do in Chapter 1, then a glance interface controller will have already been added to the interface for you.

Once the glance interface controller has been added to your storyboard, you add user interface elements like labels and images, just like with any other interface controller.

When you select the glance interface controller itself (by clicking on the yellow circle icon that appears above the interface), the Attributes Inspector of the glance's interface controller will let you choose a template layout for both parts of the glance by clicking on them (see Figure 3-2).

 You don't have to use a template, but it's something you should seriously consider. When a user starts looking at the glances provided by the apps on his watch, having a wide variety of differently laid-out interfaces can mean that he will need to spend more time adjusting to different layouts as he navigates from glance to glance. If you're making your users slow down, then you might be defeating the purpose of glances—which is to quickly provide important information.

Figure 3-2. Selecting a template to use for the glance

Providing the code for the interface controller is almost identical to any other interface controller that you have in your WatchKit app. You use outlets to connect the interface elements to properties in your code, which you use to provide content to the interface at runtime.

One important element of coding for glance interface controllers is that they are created early, and then kept in memory so that they appear almost instantly when the user needs them. When the user displays the glance, the interface controller will be presented.

This means that the interface controller's `awakeWithContext` method will be called quite some time before the `willActivate` method is called. If you're using the `awakeWithContext` method to prepare your interface with the information that needs to be shown to the user, it might be out of date by the time she sees the glance. Instead, update your interface with the information that needs to be presented inside the `willActivate` method.

Creating a Glance Scheme

To run the app and show the glance, select the Glance scheme from the scheme picker at the top left of the Xcode window (see Figure 3-3.)

Figure 3-3. Selecting the Glance scheme

This scheme is added by default if you chose to add a Glance to your app when creating the project. However, if you're adding a glance interface to your app later, you'll need to add the scheme yourself.

To do this, follow these steps:

1. Open the Scheme manager by opening the Product menu, choosing Scheme, and then choosing Manage Schemes.
2. Select the scheme for the WatchKit app.
3. Click the settings icon at the lower left, and choose Duplicate.
4. Rename the new scheme something appropriate, like "WatchKit App Glance."
5. Click the Edit button, and select the Run action.
6. In the settings for the Run action, set the Watch Interface option to `Glance`.
7. Close the scheme editor and select the new Glance scheme.

When you build and run by pressing Command-R, the Glance interface will appear. If you want to go back to the main application, simply change back to the previous scheme.

Tapping the Glance

When the user taps on your glance, the main WatchKit application is launched. The glance and the application are actually two separate executable files, and therefore are two separate processes that don't share memory.

When the app is launched from the glance, the main interface controller will be displayed. In most cases, this is exactly what you want—the user was looking at some information, and is now using your app to dig deeper.

Sometimes, however, you don't want to show the main interface contoller. For example, if you're making a calendar app and the glance shows your next meeting, you might want to display more info about that next meeting when the glance is tapped.

The way to handle this is by using the user activity API. When new data is being presented by your glance interface controller, call updateUserActivity(_, userInfo:, webpageURL:):

```swift
override func willActivate() {
        // The glance is being presented to the user.

        // Create a dictionary containing info that the main
        // app can use to display this content

        // For example, if you're making a calendar app,
        // each 'event' might have an ID number, which
        // the main app can use to look up and display full
        // information about that event.
        let info = ["calendarEventID": 99];

        // Update the activity so that, if the glance is
        // tapped, the main application will receive the
        // info dictionary
        self.updateUserActivity("au.com.secretlab." +
            "SwiftDevForAppleWatch.HelloWatch" +
            ".watchkitextension.tapped",
            userInfo: info,
            webpageURL: nil)

        super.willActivate()
    }
```

When the user taps on the glance, the main watch application will launch. Immediately after launching, the handleUserActivity() method on your WatchKit app's main interface controller will be called. This method receives the dictionary that was provided to the userInfo parameter of update user activity, and you can use this dictionary to configure your interface, or to present other interface controllers:

```swift
override func handleUserActivity(userInfo: [NSObject : AnyObject]?) {
    // We've just been launched, and WatchKit is telling
    // us about the reason why we were launched.
```

```
        // The userInfo dict contains the data that was
        // provided to updateUserActivity.
        print("Launched from user-activity (aka glance): \(userInfo)")
    }
```

You won't receive any notification that the glance is about to launch the main application. Instead, you should call `updateUserActivity` whenever you are displaying new information on the glance screen; if the user happens to tap on the glance, the main app will end up displaying the correct information.

The final glance from this chapter is shown in Figure 3-4.

Figure 3-4. The glance, running on the watch

Wrapping Up

Glances let you provide the user with a quick way to see the most important information that your app can provide. In addition to this, you can also customize the interface that's shown when the user receives a notification. We'll be looking at this in the next chapter.

CHAPTER 4

Notifications

When you receive an email, iMessage, or tweet, applications on your iPhone have the ability to show a notification on the screen. These notifications are generally limited in terms of what they can do: they can display a message, play a sound, and also update the badge number on the application's icon.

With an Apple Watch, notifications that appear on the phone are also displayed on the watch. If you don't do anything, the watch simply displays the notification message (if one is present) alongside the iOS application's icon. This means that you don't need to take your phone out of your pocket when you feel it vibrate; instead, you just need to quickly look at your watch.

However, WatchKit allows you to add more functionality to the notification system, and go beyond simply displaying a message. Your app can provide a custom interface, which takes the contents of the notification that the phone received and presents it using interface elements that are entirely under your control.

In addition to simply presenting messages, notifications can also be *actionable*. Starting in iOS 8, notifications gained the ability to have *actions*: notifications could have buttons attached to them, allowing the user to perform some task without having to unlock his phone or leave his current app. These actions can be configured to appear based on different kinds of notifications; for example, when one of your friends checks in somewhere on the location-sharing app Swarm, the notification that Swarm displays includes a button that lets you Like the check-in without having to launch Swarm itself.

It's entirely possible that most of the time users spend interacting with their watches will be with notifications, which means that if your iOS app is going to be presenting notifications to the user, you should spend at least some time considering how those notifications will look on the watch. In this chapter, you'll learn how notifications are displayed to the user, and how to create and configure your own interfaces. You'll also learn how to deal with actionable notifications, and how to let the user take action when a notification arrives.

Glances and notifications

Glances and notifications can seem quite similar, especially when we start talking about the difference between *short-look* and *long-look* notifications, which are the two types of interfaces that you design when creating a custom notification—a short-look notification only appears when you quickly glance at the watch, after all.

To be clear, a *glance* is a screen of content that appears when you swipe up from the bottom of the watch face. Glances are for providing a summary of important information that relates to an app.

A *notification* is a screen of content that appears when your phone receives a message. For example, when your phone receives an iMessage from a friend, the notification will show the text of that iMessage. When you build a custom notification, you customize this interface that appears.

Creating Notifications for Your iOS App

In order to work with notifications on the watch, it's important to first understand how notifications work on the iPhone.

Notifications can come from two different sources:

- *Remote* notifications, also known as *push* notifications, are delivered by the Apple Push Notification server to the phone.
- *Local* notifications are notifications that are scheduled by the application itself, and don't involve any communication with the Apple Push Notification server.

From the user's perspective, remote and local notifications look like the same thing: depending on the content of the notification, the user sees some alert text, hears a sound, sees a badge appear on the application icon, or some combination of the above.

Because both remote and local notifications are effectively the same from the user's perspective, the way that applications register their intent to show notifications is the same for both remote and local notifications. To begin showing notifications, follow these steps:

1. First, identify the different *categories* of notifications you plan on receiving. For example, if you were making a social networking app, you might expect to have a

notification for when the user receives a message, and another notification for when someone *likes* their post.

2. Next, for each category of notification, identify the *actions* that the user can take. To continue the social networking app example, if the user receives a message, a potential action is to reply to that message, while if someone *likes* a post, a potential action is to view the profile of that user.

3. For each action that can be taken, create a `UIMutableUserNotificationAction` and prepare it in your iOS application's application delegate's `applicationDidFi nishLaunching` method (for example, in *ApplicationDelegate.swift* in your project), like so:

```
let replyAction = UIMutableUserNotificationAction()
replyAction.identifier = "replyToMessage"
replyAction.title = "Reply"
```

Once you have the notifications you want for a category, you create a `UIMutableUser NotificationCategory`, give it an identifier, and provide it with the actions that should be attached to it. Different actions can be made available in different contexts —for example, the *default* context applies when the notification appears on the lock screen, and the *minimal* context applies in more space-constrained environments, like when the user pulls down on a notification banner:

```
let messageReceivedCategory = UIMutableUserNotificationCategory()
        messageReceivedCategory.identifier = "messageReceived"

// The default context is the lock screen.
messageReceivedCategory.setActions([replyAction],
    forContext: UIUserNotificationActionContext.Default)

// The minimal context is when the user pulls down on a notification banner.
messageReceivedCategory.setActions([replyAction],
    forContext: UIUserNotificationActionContext.Minimal)
```

 On the Apple Watch, all notifications are shown in the default context. However, you still need to think about the minimal context, because your notifications might *also* be shown on the iPhone.

Once all of the categories have been created, you need to create a `UIUserNotifica tionSettings` object. This object describes to iOS what the user will see when a notification appears; that is, if they will see a message, hear a sound, or see a badge on the app icon (or some combination of the three.) The settings object also contains the collection of category objects:

```
let settings = UIUserNotificationSettings(
    forTypes: [
```

```
        UIUserNotificationType.Alert,
        UIUserNotificationType.Badge,
        UIUserNotificationType.Sound
    ], categories: [messageReceivedCategory]
)
```

Once the settings object is prepared, you call `registerUserNotificationSettings` on the shared `UIApplication` object, like so:

```
UIApplication.sharedApplication()
    .registerUserNotificationSettings(settings)
```

At this point, the system will display the alert box that asks for permission to display alerts, play sounds, and update the badge. If the user chooses to not allow this by declining to grant permission to the app, no notifications will be shown, either on the iPhone or the watch.

 There's one additional step needed for remote notifications. Once you've registered your intent to show notifications to the user, you then need to call `registerForRemoteNotifications()` on the shared `UIApplication` object. This kicks off an additional process, in which the phone will contact the Apple Push Notification service and deliver a device identifier token to the application delegate, which your app then needs to deliver to a server that you control.

Registering for and delivering push notifications is outside of the scope of this book, as we're focusing on how the Apple Watch displays notifications in general. To learn more about how to implement remote notifications, see the Local and Remote Notification Programming Guide in the Xcode documentation (*http://bit.ly/loc-remote*).

When a notification arrives, the identifier of the notification's category is included alongside any other information, like the alert title. The category identifier is used by the system to work out which action buttons should be attached, if applicable. On the lock screen, any actions that were added to the category's *default* context are accessible by swiping on the notification right to left; if the user has unlocked her phone and a notification banner appears, any actions that were added to the category's *minimal* context appear when she pulls down on the banner.

Presenting Notifications

There are two types of interfaces that the watch presents for a notification: a short-look interface, and a long-look interface.

When a notification comes in, the watch vibrates and shows the short-look notification. If the user looks at the notification for a couple of seconds (which the watch detects based on information coming from the built-in motion sensors), the watch loads the long-look notification and presents it.

The short-look interface can't be customized. Instead, when you want to customize the way that the notification is presented to the user, you provide your own long-look interface, which replaces the default interface.

Creating Custom Notification Interfaces

The custom long-look notification interface is managed by a special of `WKInterface Controller` subclass called `WKUserNotificationInterfaceController`. This class works identically to regular interface controllers, but has two additional methods: `didReceiveRemoteNotification` and `didReceiveLocalNotification`. These methods are called when the iOS application that your WatchKit app is paired with displays a remote or local notification, and they serve as your opportunity to update the interface controller's UI elements to show useful information.

`WKUserNotificationInterfaceController` is created by the system, and may be reused for multiple notifications. This means that in the `didReceiveRemoteNotifica tion` and `didReceiveLocalNotification` methods, the interface may have already been loaded, and is about to be displayed to the user in just a moment. If this interface controller was previously used to show an earlier notification, it may contain out-of-date information. It's up to you to load the most current information being shown to the user, and you need to do so as fast as you can, or the user will see out-of-date content.

Custom long-look notification interfaces all use a similar layout. From top to bottom, the screen shows:

- The *sash*, which is a colored bar that contains the app icon and the title of the notification
- The *content area*, which is the region in which you can put your own UI content
- The bottom of the interface controller, which shows the list of buttons for each action registered with the notification, as well as a Dismiss button at the very bottom

Figure 4-1 shows a notification comprising all three of these elements. The sash shows the iMessage icon and the word "Messages," the content area shows the message itself, and beneath the content area, a Reply button appears above the standard Dismiss button.

Figure 4-1. A notification received by the Apple Watch

 You can't change the structure of this interface beyond the interface elements you put in the content area, the buttons in the bottom of the interface, and the color of the sash.

Static and Dynamic Notification Interfaces

When you create a custom long-look interface, you create at least one interface, called the *static* interface. You can also create a *dynamic* interface, which is controlled by your `WKUserInterfaceController`.

The *static* interface just shows the alert text of the notification in a `WKInterfaceLabel`, along with the list of actions, but you can customize its design by configuring the position and style of the alert label, and also by adding your own static text and images. The goal of the static interface is to allow your notifications to look like they fit in with the visual design of your parent iOS application.

The *dynamic* interface, which is optional, is a `WKUserNotificationInterfaceController` subclass that you write; in the `didReceiveRemoteNotification` and `didReceiveLocalNotification` methods, you receive the contents of the dictionary or `UILocalNotification` object that the application received (depending on whether the notification was a remote notification or a local notification), and populate the interface according to your own requirements.

The main reason for this split between static and dynamic interfaces for your custom notifications is power consumption. Launching additional code means that the Apple Watch needs to consume additional CPU resources to load, run, and manage a process on the watch that updates the interface.

As the saying goes, the best way to optimize code is to never run that code at all; if the notification is guaranteed to never need code to run, WatchKit can simply display it without having to use these extra resources. This can save a large amount of power.

Because of this, the system may decide to display the static interface even if a dynamic interface is available. If the watch is low on power, or if the code that prepares the dynamic interface takes too long to run, the system will fall back to the static interface.

It's worth keeping in mind that many notifications don't actually need a dynamic interface. Consider carefully if you really do need to update your interface from code.

Setting Up for Testing Notifications

In the real world, a notification UI is presented as a result of the iOS app receiving a notification. That can be fiddly to set up when you're developing and testing your notification interface, so Xcode provides a way to test different notifications in the Apple Watch simulator.

First, you create a file that contains the same information that the Apple Push Notification server sends to the phone. This information is represented in the human-readable JSON format. Next, in the Run action for the scheme that you use for running the Notification in the Apple Watch simulator, you select this new push notification file. When the app launches, the Apple Watch simulator is given the push notification data from the file you wrote, and uses that to display a notification.

If you chose to create a notifications interface when creating the project, you don't need to follow these steps. However, if you're adding a custom notification interface to an existing project, or if you want to test multiple different types of notifications, read on.

To create a test notification file, follow these steps:

1. Create the file by opening the File menu, and choose New→File. Select the Apple Watch category, and choose Notification Simulation File. Create the new file.

2. Customize the notification to suit your needs by opening the file and modifying the notification:

a. The `aps` dictionary contains information used by iOS and by the Apple Watch to present the static notification. The `body` key is the notification message itself, while the `title` key is optional and determines the notification title.

b. The `WatchKit Simulator Actions` dictionary is used only by the Apple Watch simulator, and allows you to control which actions are attached to the notification.

Actions are handled in this way when using simulated notifications, because when real notifications are delivered to the phone, the iOS app is responsible for determining which actions are attached to different notifications. When using simulated notifications, like we're doing here, there's no iOS app to provide info about which actions apply, so you need to add them yourself.

3. Any other keys you add are available for your code to use, and are delivered inside the dictionary that `handleRemoteNotification` receives as a parameter.

To test notifications in the Apple Watch simulator, you need to add a new scheme that makes the simulator display a notification. This is very similar to adding a scheme for the glance interface (see "Creating a Glance Scheme" on page 42).

1. Open the Scheme manager by opening the Product menu, choosing Scheme, and then choosing Manage Schemes.

2. Select the scheme for the WatchKit app.

3. Click the settings icon at the lower left, and choose Duplicate.

4. Rename the new scheme something appropriate, like "WatchKit App Notification."

5. Click the Edit button, and select the Run action.

6. In the settings for the Run action, set the Watch Interface option to `Notification`.

7. Set the Notification Payload to the file you just created.

8. Close the scheme editor, and select the new Notification scheme.

Creating the Interface Controller

If you want to customize the long-look interface for your notifications, you need to create and configure an interface controller. To do this, follow these steps:

1. Create a subclass of `WKUserNotificationInterfaceController:` from the File menu, choose New→File, choose the Source category, and create a new Cocoa Touch subclass.

Make the *Subclass of* be `WKUserNotificationInterfaceController`.

2. Add a new notification interface controller to the storyboard by opening your app's main storyboard and dragging in a new notification interface controller from the Object Library. This will add the static interface for the notification.

3. Select the arrow that's connected to the interface. In the Attributes Inspector, set the Name of the category to the identifier of one of the `UIMutableUserNotifica tionCategory` objects that the iOS app registers for.

 If you don't specify a notification category, and instead just leave it blank, then the notification interface will be used as the "default" interface, and will appear for all notifications that don't have their own specific notification interface controllers.

You create multiple notification interface controllers, one for each different notification category your app has. If you have more than one category, simply drag in multiple notification interface controllers, and configure each category to use the appropriate identifier in the Name field.

By default, a notification interface controller only has the static interface, and it doesn't use the `WKUserNotificationInterfaceController` subclass. Again, it's worth remembering that many notifications don't need a code-driven interface. If you decide that you don't need to add a dynamic interface, you can skip the first step of this process, and just add the static interface.

If you do decide that you need a dynamic interface, follow these steps:

1. Select the notification category arrow, and turn on "Has Dynamic Interface" in the Attributes Inspector. A new interface will appear, connected to the static interface.

2. Select the dynamic interface, and then select the interface controller by clicking on the yellow circular icon. Open the Identity Inspector, and in the Class field, type the name of your `WKUserNotificationInterfaceController`. Once that's done, you can set up your interface controller just like any other, by dragging controls into the interface and connecting them via outlets.

Finally, your `WKUserNotificationInterfaceController` class needs to add methods that run when a notification is received.

Implement `didReceiveLocalNotification` and `didReceiveRemoteNotification` (these methods are run when a local or remote notification is received by the iOS app, and receive the notification info as well as a completion block). After you finish using the notification info to set up your dynamic interface, you call the completion block to signal that WatchKit should use a dynamic interface:

```
override func didReceiveLocalNotification(
    localNotification: UILocalNotification, withCompletion
    completionHandler: ((WKUserNotificationInterfaceType) -> Void)) {
    // The iOS app received a local notification; set up our interface

    // When done, call completionHandler and pass .Custom.
    completionHandler(.Custom)
}

override func didReceiveRemoteNotification(
    remoteNotification: [NSObject : AnyObject], withCompletion
    completionHandler: ((WKUserNotificationInterfaceType) -> Void)) {
    // The iOS app received a local notification; set up our interface

    // When done, call completionHandler and pass .Custom.
    completionHandler(.Custom)
}
```

 If you don't call the completion block fast enough—in about a quarter of a second or less—the system will fall back to using the static interface. This means that you don't have time to talk to the network, for example, before calling the completion block.

The notification from this chapter is shown in Figure 4-2.

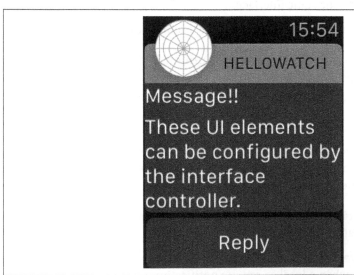

Figure 4-2. The custom long-look notification, running on the watch

Wrapping Up

If your iOS app receives notifications, creating a custom notification interface for the watchOS app can go a long way toward improving the user experience. When you create a custom notification interface, you have full control over what the user sees, and can provide much more useful information than the default interface can provide.

In the next chapter, we'll look at another feature that lets you get the most important information to the user: complications!

CHAPTER 5

Complications

With all of the other features built into the Apple Watch, it's easy to forget that it's a wristwatch at heart. Out of all of the other screens that are present in the watch, the one that will be viewed the most is the watch face: that screen that shows the time.

However, good watches do more than just show the time. They show the date, the weather, a stopwatch, and more (see Figure 5-1). These little gadgets on the clockfaces are called *complications*, so named because their original implementation in clockwork-based watches dramatically complicated the internals of the watch.

Figure 5-1. Several complications on the watch face (except for the watch dial and hands, everything in this image is a complication)

On the Apple Watch, the user can select a variety of different watch faces, and some faces can include complications. These complications include things like the date, the next event on the calendar, and so on; you can see an example of several complications in Figure 5-1. Your watchOS applications can provide complications as well, and in this chapter, we'll look at how to create them.

Designing a Complication

Before we set out to build a complication, it's worth taking a moment to discuss what a complication is *for*. Because they're shown on the watch face, a complication's role is focused on time. A complication needs to present some time-related data to the user; for example, the Weather complication shows the current weather, the Calendar complication shows the next event, and so on.

Not all apps need to have a complication. If the content presented by your app isn't *timely*—that is, it can't be linked to a specific date and time—consider not including one.

Content being timely doesn't necessarily mean that it directly relates to time, like a calendar entry does. For example, it makes sense for the weather complication to be a complication because it shows the current weather *right now*, and Time Travel allows you to see *future* predictions of the weather.

If your app's content can't be meaningfully discussed in terms of the data that it presents now and the data it will present in an hour's time, you may want to reconsider whether your app should provide a complication.

Building complications for apps means taking into consideration a number of design constraints that the Apple Watch faces. A typical user will look at the watch several times a day, but each time will only look at it for a few seconds—often for less than a second. This means that any information that the complication needs to display must be *already ready to show*; the watch doesn't have time to wake up your app to let it determine what to show.

On top of this, there's a reasonable chance that when the watch determines that it should wake up and show the watch face, the user isn't even looking at the watch. This means that it doesn't make sense for your watch to spend much energy preparing the content, because it may not be delivered.

When you're making a complication, you don't provide a design for its interface. Instead, you use one of several pre-prepared templates for content; these can show text, images, or a combination of the two. The specific templates that you can use depend on which *family* of complication you're providing content to.

Finally, the last thing to consider is *Time Travel*. When a user rotates the Digital Crown, the time shown on the clock face changes; the watch then shows what the screen would look like if it were the selected time. This lets the user scroll through what's coming up, or scroll back to see what conditions were like a little while ago. Of course, this is only possible if you can predict what a complication will be showing in the future; a complication that shows your most recently received email can't participate in Time Travel, because you can't know what email you'll receive next. However, the Weather app *can* participate in Time Travel, because predictions can be made ahead of time.

You can see a screenshot of Time Travel in action in Figure 5-2. In this image, time has been wound forward by nine hours; as a result, several complications have changed from their former state that reflected the present.

Figure 5-2. Time Travel in action

You'll notice that the watch dial has changed to reflect the new time, along with the date and the time shown in the other country; additionally, the temperature has changed, because what's being shown is the prediction of what the temperature *will be* in nine hours' time. Note also that the battery level at the top left has become dimmed, because the Apple Watch isn't able to predict what the battery level will be with any reasonable degree of confidence.

These design constraints mean that building a complication is significantly different than building any other part of your watchOS app. When you build the app, you're building interface controllers that present a user interface and supply it with data, one screen at a time. When you design a constraint, however, you're *only* supplying data;

additionally, if you're participating in Time Travel (and you should), then you supply *multiple* pieces of data.

The Data Provider

When your app provides a complication, you create a class that conforms to the CLKComplicationDataSource protocol. This protocol defines the methods that watchOS will call in order to get data from your app for display on the watch face.

You don't actually create an instance of this class; instead, you provide the name of the class in your project settings, and watchOS will instantiate the class when it needs to.

Because a complication's entire purpose is to provide timely information, all data shown on the watch face is tied to a specific moment in time. These are represented by *timeline entries*: objects that contain information to be shown to the user, alongside the specific time and date at which point the information is correct.

The data provider object's purpose is to respond to requests from watchOS for timeline entries. Complications always have at least one timeline entry, but they can often have more than one. This is how Time Travel works; when a complication is loaded, watchOS asks the complication's data source class for as many timeline entries as possible, so that when the user rotates the Digital Crown, the appropriate timeline entry can be displayed.

The data source class is repeatedly asked for more timeline entries as time goes by. The specific times are controlled by watchOS, in order to make sure that there's timely information, ready to display, the moment the user looks at the watch face.

 The data source is expected to respond to queries as fast as possible. Don't access the network or query the device. If the data that your complication needs to provide comes from the network, your iOS app or main watchOS app should query the data ahead of time, and store it somewhere that the complication can access it. This is a bit beyond the scope of this chapter, but for more information, see the "Leveraging iOS Technologies" section in the App Programming Guide for watchOS (*http://bit.ly/leverage-ios*).

Adding a complication to an existing project. If you followed the instructions in Chapter 2, your project will already be set up to provide a complication. If you're working with an existing project that you want to add a complication to, you can add it by following these steps:

1. Add a new file to your project by opening the File menu and choosing New→File. Create a new Cocoa Touch Class, and make it a subclass of NSObject.

2. In the newly created file, make the file conform to the `CLKComplicationData` `Source` protocol:

```
class ComplicationController: NSObject,
    CLKComplicationDataSource {
```

3. Select your project at the top of the Project Navigator.
4. Select the WatchKit Extension in the list of targets.
5. Scroll down to the Complications Configuration section of the page, and set the Data Source Class to the class you just created (see Figure 5-3).
6. For the example in this chapter, turn on the Utilitarian Large family in the list of checkboxes.

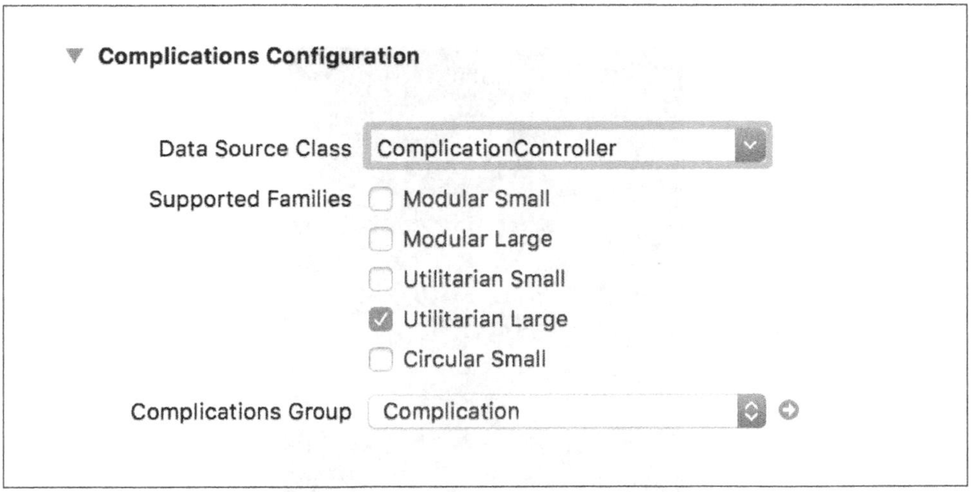

Figure 5-3. Configuring a project to have a complication

Templates and Timelines

To show information to the user, a timeline entry uses a *template*. A template is an object that contains text, images, or both, and watchOS provides a number of different types of templates. You can't create your own custom templates; instead, you use the templates that are available to you.

Different templates are available for different complication *families*. Each watch face is capable of displaying different types of complications; however, it doesn't make a lot of sense to have to create a new complication for each of the available watch faces. Instead, complications are grouped into families of different shapes and sizes, and each watch face can support different families.

This means that your complications need to be designed for specific families; if you create a complication that supports only the Utilitarian Large and Utilitarian Small families, your complication won't be available on the Modular watch face. You can make your complication support all available families, but doing so requires specific code for each family that you support.

Building a Complication

Because complications are, well, a little complicated, we'll work through an example complication from start to finish. This complication, which will work with the Utilitarian watch face, displays the name of the next meal; for example, if you look at your watch early in the morning, it will say "breakfast," around noon it will say "lunch," and in the evening it will say "supper." You can see a screenshot of the complication in Figure 5-4.

Figure 5-4. The demo complication we'll be building in this chapter

 This section assumes your data source class is called Complication Controller, because that's the name of the file that Xcode creates if you choose to add a complication when creating a project.

To get started, we'll first create some code that isn't specifically related to complications, but will provide us with the data that the complication will show. Specifically, we need to think about the data that the complication will present.

Overthinking Our Food

Let's stop thinking about the Apple Watch for a moment, and think about how daily meals work. In most Western cultures, there are three main meals per day: breakfast, lunch, and dinner. There are also several *other* meals: a midnight snack, afternoon tea, elevenses, and so on. All of these usually happen at a particular time: breakfast is eaten in the morning—say, around 7AM—while dinner is eaten in the evening.

However, there's a distinction that needs to be made between a general *kind* of meal, like evening dinners, and a *specific* meal, like the one that you'll hopefully have tomorrow tonight. Meals repeat: you had breakfast yesterday, hopefully, and all things going well, you'll have one tomorrow. Specific *meal occurrences* happen only once: the breakfast that I had this morning has already happened, and will never happen again.

The data that's shown in a complication relates to this second kind of data: specific events, which are shown on the watch face. The Apple Watch needs to know about the precise date of the event, so that when a user glances at his wrist, he can immediately be shown the correct information.

This means that we have two separate kinds of data in the app: Meals and MealOccurrences. A Meal is simply an association between a meal's name and the hour of the day it will occur, while a MealOccurrence is the name of a meal and a specific NSDate. We *could* create classes for these two different types, but because we're just working with some pretty simple data, we can also use tuples for the same effect and with quite a bit less typing.

Implementing the Complication

To get started, we'll first implement the data structures that the complication will work with, along with the code that provides the necessary data:

1. Open *ComplicationController.swift*.

2. If there's any code in the ComplicationController class, delete it. (The template file that comes with the project contains a number of placeholder methods; we'll be writing all of ours from scratch.)

3. Add the following code to the ComplicationController class:

   ```
   // A "Meal" is an hour of the day, and the name of
   // the meal to eat at that hour.
   typealias Meal = (hour: Int, name: String)

   // A MealOccurrence is a specific meal that's eaten
   // at a specific date and time.
   typealias MealOccurrence = (name: String, date: NSDate)
   ```

We can now define the list of meals that happen over the course of the day. We'll store this as an array of Meals.

Add the following array to ComplicationController:

```
// Define the list of meals.
let meals : [Meal] = [
    (7, "Breakfast"),
    (9, "Second Breakfast"),
    (10, "Brunch"),
    (11, "Elevenses"),
    (13, "Lunch"),
    (16, "Tea"),
    (19, "Dinner"),
    (21, "Supper"),
    (23, "Snack")
]
```

Now that each meal has an associated hour of the day, we can write code that uses the meals list to determine the next MealOccurrence—the name of the next meal, and the time at which it should be eaten—that will happen after a specified date:

```
func nextMealOccurrenceAfterDate(date: NSDate) -> MealOccurrence {
    // Determine the next MealOccurrence that happens after the provided date.

    let calendar = NSCalendar.currentCalendar()

    // Determine the date's hour value.
    let hour = calendar.components(NSCalendarUnit.Hour, fromDate: date).hour

    // Find the next Meal whose hour is after this date's hour.
    var selectedMeal : Meal? = nil

    for meal in meals  {
        if meal.hour > hour {
            selectedMeal = meal
            break
        }
    }

    // Stores the calculated date of this next meal's occurrence.
    var mealDate : NSDate

    if selectedMeal == nil {

        // No more meals take place today. The next meal will be the first
        // meal that occurs tomorrow.
        selectedMeal = meals[0]
    }

    // Calculate the date for this meal.

    // Start by getting a new date where the time is set to the start of
    // the meal's hour
    mealDate = calendar.dateBySettingHour(
        selectedMeal!.hour, minute: 0, second: 0,
        ofDate: NSDate(), options: [])!
```

```
        // If this date is *before* the specified date...
        if mealDate.earlierDate(date) == mealDate {
            // ...then we've wrapped around to the start of the day.
            // We should add one day to the date.
            mealDate = calendar.dateByAddingUnit(
                .Day, value: 1, toDate: mealDate, options: [])!
        }

        // Return the MealOccurrence - its name, and the time at which it's eaten.
        return (selectedMeal!.name, mealDate)
    }
```

Presenting the Complication

Now that we have a source of time-related information to show, we can start presenting data in the complication.

The visible thing that a complication displays is called a *template*. At runtime, watchOS will ask the data provider class to create and prepare a timeline entry, which consists of a template paired with an NSDate. For this complication, we'll implement a method that prepares a template based on a given date. This isn't part of the CLKCom plicationDataSource protocol, but because it'll be called from multiple places, it's best to put it in a separate method.

When you create a template for display in a complication, you need to give it the data that it needs to show. This is done through *text providers* and *image providers*. A text provider shows either a string or a date in the complication, while an image provider displays an image. Different providers do different things; for example, the CLKSimple TextProvider just shows a string of text, while a CLKTimeTextProvider shows the time value in an NSDate.

Different kinds of templates support different types of providers. For example, the CLKComplicationTemplateCircularSmallSimpleText template can display a single text provider, while larger, more complex templates like CLKComplicationTemplateMo dularLargeColumns support up to six text providers or three image providers.

In this complication, we'll use the CLKComplicationTemplateUtilitarianLargeFlat template, which can present either a single text provider or a single image provider. We'll give it a text provider to show the name of the next MealOccurrence.

 Importantly, the method that prepares a template given a MealOc currence will also support being given a nil value. This will be used later, when watchOS needs a template to show in the compli cation before any data has been requested yet.

Add the following method to the `ComplicationController` class:

```
func templateForMeal(mealOccurrence : MealOccurrence?,
    inComplication complication: CLKComplication) -> CLKComplicationTemplate {

    // Given a meal occurrence, creates and prepares a complication template.

    // Different complication families require different kinds of templates.
    // If you want to support different families, add more cases to this
    // switch statement.

    let mealName = mealOccurrence?.name ?? "Next Meal"

    switch complication.family {
    case .UtilitarianLarge:

        // Create the template
        let t = CLKComplicationTemplateUtilitarianLargeFlat()

        t.textProvider = CLKSimpleTextProvider(
            text: mealName)

        return t;
    default:
        fatalError("Unsupported complication family: \(complication.family)")
    }

}
```

Creating Timeline Entries

Now that we have templates to show, we simply need to create timeline entries when watchOS requests them. There are a few methods that are part of the `CLKComplicationDataSource` protocol that are required:

- `getSupportedTimeTravelDirectionsForComplication` is called to determine what time travel directions are supported, if any; that is, if the complication should appear if Time Travel is showing a time in the future, or if it's showing a time in the past

- `getCurrentTimelineEntryForComplication` is called to get the current timeline entry

- `getPlaceholderTemplateForComplication` is called to get a template to show on the selection screen; it doesn't need to show actual data, but rather should show some placeholder information

The second method, `getCurrentTimelineEntryForComplication`, is responsible for returning the *current* timeline entry. This is the timeline entry that the user will see when she glances at her wrist (and when she's not using Time Travel.)

Add the following method to `ComplicationController`:

```swift
func getCurrentTimelineEntryForComplication(complication: CLKComplication,
    withHandler handler: (CLKComplicationTimelineEntry?) -> Void) {

    // Provides the current entry on the timeline.

    // Get the current date.
    let date = NSDate()

    // Get the next meal that happens after this date.
    let meal = nextMealOccurrenceAfterDate(date)

    // Get the template for this meal occurrence.
    let template = templateForMeal(meal, inComplication: complication)

    // Create an entry using this date and template.
    let entry = CLKComplicationTimelineEntry(date: date,
                                            complicationTemplate: template)

    // Provide it to watchOS.
    handler(entry)

}
```

Once you have a template, you construct a timeline entry by creating an instance of the `CLKComplicationTimelineEntry` class. This simply combines the date of the timeline entry with the template to use.

 You might notice that we don't return this value. Instead, the method receives a `handler` closure to call, which takes the template as a parameter. You need to call this closure before the method exits.

Next, we'll implement the method that returns the *placeholder* template. This template is used on the selection screen, before any data is loaded.

Add the following method to `ComplicationController`:

```swift
func getPlaceholderTemplateForComplication(complication: CLKComplication,
    withHandler handler: (CLKComplicationTemplate?) -> Void) {

    // Provides a placeholder template for the complication, used in the
    // complication selection screen.

    // Passing in 'nil' here because we're not actually trying to
    // show information, we just want the placeholder template.
    let template = templateForMeal(nil, inComplication: complication)
```

```
    handler(template)
}
```

In this method, we aren't creating a timeline entry; instead, we're just returning a static template to show.

Supporting Time Travel

Finally, we'll implement support for Time Travel. To be specific, we'll make this complication capable of *future* time travel; that is, the user can Time Travel into the future and see what future meals will be.

Doing this involves two steps: first, we indicate to watchOS that this complication is capable of participating in Time Travel, and second, we implement a method that returns the list of *future* timeline entries that should be shown when the user Time Travels.

Add the following method to ComplicationController:

```
func getSupportedTimeTravelDirectionsForComplication(
    complication: CLKComplication,
    withHandler handler: (CLKComplicationTimeTravelDirections) -> Void) {
    // Provides the direction of time travel that this complication can do.
    // In this case, we support forward time travel.
    handler([.Forward])
}
```

Complications can also indicate that they support backward time travel by returning .Backward in the list passed to the completion handler. Complications can also indicate that they support *both* forward and backward time travel by returning a list that contains both .Forward and .Backward.

Next, add the following method to ComplicationController:

```
func getTimelineEntriesForComplication(complication: CLKComplication,
    afterDate date: NSDate, limit: Int,
        withHandler handler: ([CLKComplicationTimelineEntry]?) -> Void) {

    // Provides the list of timeline entries that will take place in the
    // future.

    var timelineEntries : [CLKComplicationTimelineEntry] = []

    // We'll create the list of timeline entries by figuring out the next meal
    // after nextMealDate, and then setting nextMealDate to that next
    // meal's date. We can then repeat the process.
    var nextMealDate = date

    // We've been asked to create no more than 'limit' entries.
```

```
for _ in 0..<limit {

    // Get the next meal after nextMealDate
    let nextOccurrence = nextMealOccurrenceAfterDate(nextMealDate)

    // Create the template and timeline entry for this meal
    let template = templateForMeal(
        nextOccurrence, inComplication: complication)
    let entry = CLKComplicationTimelineEntry(
        date: nextOccurrence.date, complicationTemplate: template)

    // Add it to the list
    timelineEntries.append(entry)

    // Next meal should be after this meal's date
    nextMealDate = nextOccurrence.date

}

// Provide the list to watchOS
handler(timelineEntries)

}
```

This method is responsible for providing an array of timeline entries, each of which must be after the provided `date`. No more than `limit` entries should be returned.

The method creates this list by repeatedly calculating the next meal occurrence after the `date`; once it has the next meal, it stores its date, and then looks for the *next* meal after this date. This continues until `limit` timeline entries have been created.

 If your complication supports backward Time Travel, you will need to implement `getTimelineEntriesForComplication(complication: CLKComplication, beforeDate: NSDate, limit: Int, withHandler:)` as well—this method returns a list of timeline entries in the past.

With that, the complication is ready, and you can now test it! Open the Scheme chooser, and select the Complication scheme from the list. Then click the Play button, or press Command-R to build and run the app. The Watch simulator will open, but instead of showing your app, the watch face will appear.

To test your complication, you'll need to add it to the simulator's watch face. On the Apple Watch, you do this by pressing hard on the watch face, which opens the watch face chooser; you then select the watch face you want to use, tap Configure, and then choose which complications should appear.

You do a similar thing on the simulator, but with one main difference—instead of pressing hard in real life, you tell the simulator whether you want to perform a shallow press or a deep press by pressing Command-Shift-1 and Command-Shift-2:

1. Press Command-Shift-2 to switch to Deep Press mode.

2. Tap the watch face, and the watch face chooser will appear.

3. Press Command-Shift-1 to switch back to Shallow Press mode.

4. Switch to the Utility watch face.

5. Tap Customize.

6. There are three pages of customizations that can be made to the Utility watch-face; swipe from right to left until you reach the third and final one.

7. Tap the complication at the bottom of the watch face, and scroll the trackpad (if you have one) or your mouse until you find your complication.

8. Press Command-Shift-H to simulate pressing the Digital Crown, and you'll return to the watch face chooser screen. Press it again, and you'll return to the watch face.

9. Scroll your trackpad or mouse to activate Time Travel. The complication will show future meals.

Wrapping Up

Complications provide you with an incredibly powerful way to let your user see information that's most useful to them. Because your app provides the data well in advance of the user seeing it, the watch is able to very quickly show the latest information; additionally, through Time Travel, the user can peek ahead and see what's coming up, or what's happened in the past.

Index

About the Authors

Dr. Jon Manning and **Dr. Paris Buttfield-Addison** are cofounders of the game and app development studio Secret Lab. They're based on the side of a mountain in Hobart, Tasmania, Australia.

Through Secret Lab, they've worked on award-winning apps of all sorts, ranging from iPad games for children to instant-messaging clients to math games about frogs. Together they've written numerous books on game development, iOS software development, and Mac software development. Secret Lab can be found online (*http://www.secretlab.com.au*) and on Twitter at @thesecretlab (*http://www.twitter.com/thesecretlab*).

Paris has a BA in medieval history, a BComp with first class honors, and a PhD in computing/HCI, where he focused on the use of tablet technology.

Jon has a BComp with first class honors, and a PhD in computing/HCI, where he explored manipulation on social media sites.

Paris and Jon formerly worked with Meebo (which was acquired by Google) as product manager and senior software engineer, respectively. Both have written more than a dozen technical, game design, and mobile development books, mostly for O'Reilly Media. Paris can be found on Twitter at @parisba (*http://twitter.com/parisba*) and Jon can be found at @desplesda (*https://twitter.com/desplesda*).

Colophon

The animal on the cover of *Swift Development for the Apple Watch* is an alpine swift (*Tachymarptis melba*). The fastest member of the swift family, alpine swifts are native to southern Europe and the Himalayas and migrate as far as southern Africa.

Although alpine swifts have very short legs that are useful for clinging to rocky surfaces, they prefer never to settle on the ground. Instead, swifts spend the majority of their lives in the air and can stay aloft for up to six months at a time. All essential functions—eating, drinking, and sleeping—can be performed during flight.

The need to roost is the only thing that will compel an alpine swift to land, and they prefer to build their nests on the sides of cliffs or mountains. Alpine swifts pair for life and will return to the same sites year after year to rebuild and repair nests. Swifts have taken well to the development of cities along the Mediterranean, where old buildings provide excellent spaces for roosting and laying eggs.

Many of the animals on O'Reilly covers are endangered; all of them are important to the world. To learn more about how you can help, go to *animals.oreilly.com*.

The cover image is from Wood's *Illustrated Natural History*. The cover fonts are URW Typewriter and Guardian Sans. The text font is Adobe Minion Pro; the heading font is Adobe Myriad Condensed; and the code font is Dalton Maag's Ubuntu Mono.

Get even more for your money.

Join the O'Reilly Community, and register the O'Reilly books you own. It's free, and you'll get:

- $4.99 ebook upgrade offer
- 40% upgrade offer on O'Reilly print books
- Membership discounts on books and events
- Free lifetime updates to ebooks and videos
- Multiple ebook formats, DRM FREE
- Participation in the O'Reilly community
- Newsletters
- Account management
- 100% Satisfaction Guarantee

Signing up is easy:

1. Go to: oreilly.com/go/register
2. Create an O'Reilly login.
3. Provide your address.
4. Register your books.

Note: English-language books only

To order books online:
oreilly.com/store

For questions about products or an order:
orders@oreilly.com

To sign up to get topic-specific email announcements and/or news about upcoming books, conferences, special offers, and new technologies:
elists@oreilly.com

For technical questions about book content:
booktech@oreilly.com

To submit new book proposals to our editors:
proposals@oreilly.com

O'Reilly books are available in multiple DRM-free ebook formats. For more information:
oreilly.com/ebooks

O'REILLY®

Have it your way.

Lightning Source UK Ltd.
Milton Keynes UK
UKOW05f2324030616

275542UK00002B/3/P